MOTORCYCLING: THE COMPLETE GUIDE

MOTORCYCLING

The Complete Guide

Jennifer D. Robbins
Peter W. Robbins
Gail Lucas

Illustrations by Clair Hodgson

Shaw & Sons Limited

Published by Shaw & Sons Limited
Shaway House
21 Bourne Park
Bourne Road
Crayford
Kent DA1 4BZ

First published 1991

ISBN 0 7219 1260 5

Printed in Great Britain by BPCC Wheatons Ltd, Exeter

Contents

Foreword 9

Introduction 11

1. Becoming a Motorcyclist 13
Driving licences 13
Vehicle groups 13
Conditions of a provisional licence 14
Provisional driving licence restrictions 15
How to apply for a driving licence with a motorcycle or moped entitlement 15
Duration of driving licences 16
Types of machines available 16
Mopeds 16
Scooters 17
Motorcycles 19
Motorcycles with sidecars 20
Three-wheeled vehicles 21
How to choose your machine 22
Buying a second-hand machine 23
On the road 24
Is your machine legal? 24
Documents required 24

2. Equipment and Clothing 26
Safety equipment needed 26
Legal requirements 26
Safety helmets 26
Visors and goggles 27
Glasses 28
Suitable clothing 28
General rules 28
Gloves 29
Jackets 30
Trousers 30
Footwear 30
Waterproof clothing 30

3. Maintenance and Safety 32
Keeping a machine in a roadworthy condition 32
Cleaning and polishing 32
Daily safety checks 33
Weekly checks 34
Adjusting a machine to individual requirements 35
Be safe - be seen 36
Why motorcyclists are vulnerable 36
How to be seen 36

4. Motorcycle Training 38
Compulsory basic training (CBT) 38
About the certificate 38
Types of training schemes 39
Contents of an approved training course 42
Trainee records 44
Is further training necessary? 44

5. The D.S.A. Accompanied Rider Test 48
About the motorcycle test 48
How the examiner conducts the motorcycle test 48
The start of your test 49
How the Motorcycle Accompanied Rider Test is marked 50
The result of the D.S.A. Accompanied Rider Test 55
Requirements of the D.S.A. Motorcycle Accompanied Rider Test 59
1. *The eyesight test* 59
2. *The Highway Code* 59
3. *Checks before starting the engine* 61
4. *Using the controls* 61
5. *Moving off* 64
6. *Emergency stop* 65
7. *Reversing exercise* 66
8. *Turning in the road (U-turn)* 67
9. *Reverse park* 67
10. *Using the mirrors/rear observation* 67
11. *Giving signals* 68
12. *Acting on signs and signals* 69

13. *Care in the use of speed* 70
14. *Making progress* 70
15. *Road junctions (including roundabouts)* 71
16. *Overtaking, meeting and crossing the path of other vehicles* 73
17. *Position on the road* 74
18. *Passing stationary vehicles* 75
19. *At pedestrian crossings* 75
20. *Selecting a safe position for normal stops* 76
21. *Awareness and anticipation* 76

6. A–Z of Safe Riding Skills and Techniques 78
Accident procedure 78
Bends 83
Distractions 84
Eyesight 85
Fitness to ride 85
Flood water 86
Fog code 87
Headlights 88
Horn 88
Junction procedure 89
Loads 91
Mirrors 91
Motorway riding 92
Night riding 97
Observation 98
Parking 99
Passing stationary vehicles 99
Pillion passengers 100
Rain 100
Road surfaces 101
Separation distances 102
Signals 102
Skidding 103
Snow and ice 105
Speed and speed limits 106
Tyres 107
Wind 108
Zebra (pedestrian) and pelican crossings 108

Foreword

Jenny and Peter Robbins have over 40 years' driving experience and run two driving schools in Ross-on-Wye, Herefordshire. Both are D.S.A. Approved Driving Instructors and both hold the Diploma of Driving Instruction, which is awarded jointly by the Associated Examining Board and the Driving Instructors Association. Only a small percentage of driving instructors possess this qualification. Peter is also a DIAmond Advanced Instructor.

The Robbins have written three popular driving books: 'Driving Test Questions and Answers' and 'How To Pass Your Driving Test' for learner drivers; and 'Be An Advanced Driver', which is a comprehensive reference source for anyone wishing to improve their driving to advanced standard.

Gail Lucas, co-author of this book, has had over 18 years' experience teaching all aspects of safe riding skills to motorcyclists. Prior to the introduction of the Department of Transport Part 1 Motorcycle test, Gail taught motorcylists under the RAC/ACU training scheme. When this was disbanded, she joined the British Motorcyclists Federation.

Gail is Chief Motorcycle Instructor and Course Organiser in Ross-on-Wye. She organises training schemes which include instruction to the standard required by the D.S.A. Accompanied Rider Test that learner motorcyclists and moped riders must pass to obtain a full motorcycle or moped licence.

Gail took part in the BBC TV road safety series 'Mind How You Go' with Jimmy Savile, and taught a presenter from the BBC TV programme 'That's Life' to ride a moped. In her spare time she helps to run the family motorcycle business and specialises in supplying customers worldwide with parts for Classic motorcycles.

Clair Hodgson attended Herefordshire College of Art, Middlesex Polytechnic and The Royal College of Art. She has a workshop in Herefordshire where she teaches painting and drawing, craft and jewellery making and exhibits and sells her own work throughout the world. Clair was taught to drive by Peter and Jenny Robbins and this association has led to her providing the amusing illustrations for this book.

Introduction

This book is a comprehensive reference source for riders of mopeds, scooters and motorcycles. It covers all aspects of motorcycling, from obtaining a provisional licence to details of safe riding techniques. As such, it is an invaluable guide for both novice and experienced rider alike.

The Driving Standards Agency (DSA) is an agency of the Department of Transport and is responsible for all driving tests. This publication describes what a D.S.A. examiner is looking for during the D.S.A. Accompanied Rider Test which replaced part 2 of the Motorcycle Test in October 1989, how the test is conducted and the marking system used. However, the information in this section should be read by full licence holders as well as learners, as there is much useful advice to help improve riding skills.

Test candidates for the D.S.A. Accompanied Rider Test should study the Highway Code. 'Driving Test Questions and Answers', also by Peter and Jenny Robbins, explains in detail the part of the test in which Highway Code questions are asked and contains over 200 questions in an easy-to-test-yourself format.

1. Becoming a Motorcyclist

DRIVING LICENCES

Vehicle groups (Note. This list is not comprehensive)

New EC *Code*

- ☐ A Motorbicycle (with or without sidecar) or scooter.
- ☐ B Motor car or light goods vehicle up to 9 seats/3.5 tonnes.
- ☐ B (fitted with automatic transmission). As above but with automatic transmission.
- ☐ B1 Motor tricycle or 3 wheeled car or van up to 500kg.
- ☐ C1 Goods vehicles 3.5–7.5 tonnes.
- ☐ D Large passenger carrying vehicles.
- ☐ D1 Passenger carrying vehicles with 10–17 seats.
- ☐ P British (category E) mopeds.

NB. Scooters are classified as either A or P, depending on the cubic capacity of the engine.

Old UK *code*

- ☐ A Manual gear change – car, van or truck not included in other groups.
- ☐ B Automatic transmission – car, van or truck as above.
- ☐ C Three-wheeled vehicle, (motor-tricycle).
- ☐ D Motorcycle over 50cc – with or without a sidecar.
- ☐ E Moped not exceeding 50cc. Limited to 30mph or under.
- ☐ J Invalid carriage driven by a disabled driver.

The term 'disabled driver' means one who is in possession of an invalidity or mobility allowance and whose vehicle can be adapted to take account of their disabilities and facilitate safe driving. Normally, a disabled driver's disabilities would prevent that person riding a two-wheeled machine. Cars can be adapted in a variety of ways to provide the mobility and comfort many disabled drivers require.

Conditions of a provisional licence

☐ *Age.* The legal minimum age requirements are: moped – 16 years; motorcycle – 17 years; three-wheeled vehicles – 17 years.

☐ *Eyesight.* Riders must be able to read a vehicle registration plate containing letters and figures 79.4mm high at a distance of 20.5 metres (with the aid of glasses or contact lenses if needed), in good daylight.

☐ *Health.* Riders must not suffer from a disability which would affect safe riding. All disabilities, except temporary ones lasting three months or less, must be declared.

☐ *Legal.* The provisional licence is only valid if the correct fee has been paid, it is signed in ink and the holder is not disqualified from riding or driving.

A provisional motorcycle entitlement will last two years from the original date of issue of the licence or, where the entitlement has been added to the licence afterwards, from the date of the entitlement. This will be extended for a further year if the holder has taken but failed a D.S.A. Accompanied Rider Test before the end of the entitlement or has booked a test which was not taken for a good reason, for example due to bad weather or the absence of the examiner. A provisional moped entitlement will normally last until the licence expires.

From 1 December 1990, new moped and motorcycle learner riders must take a compulsory training course (CBT) provided by an Approved Training Body before being allowed to ride a machine on the road unsupervised. Riders will be issued with a Certificate of Completion (DL196) on the successful completion of the course and this will validate the provisional motorcycle entitlement. (See Chapter 4 – Training.)

☐ *Engine capacity*. Mopeds must not exceed 50cc. Motorcycles must not exceed 125cc. Motor-tricycles must not exceed 500kg.

Provisional driving licence restrictions

☐ Regulation size L-plates must be displayed on the front and rear of the machine to be ridden.

☐ A learner rider must not ride on motorways.

☐ A learner rider must not carry a pillion passenger or sidecar passengers.

How to apply for a driving licence with a motorcycle or moped entitlement

Use Form D1 obtainable at Post Offices and give four weeks' notice. You may apply two months before you wish to use the licence. Answer questions correctly, as false information may render a person liable to prosecution.

☐ Drivers holding a full licence which covers them to drive other groups of vehicles as learners do not need a separate provisional licence for those groups, except when an older licence was issued without the motorcycle entitlement.

☐ Tick the box 'Provisional with motorcycle entitlement' if you wish to ride a moped or motorcycle. *Do not apply for this entitlement on a driving licence until you are ready to use it.*

The entitlement on the licence will be validated on successful completion of compulsory basic training (CBT).

Duration of driving licences

- ☐ Licences are issued until a person is 70 years old, unless he or she is aged 67 or over at application, in which case the licence will be issued for three years.
- ☐ When a disability has been declared, the licence is issued for one to three years. Renewal is subject to the disability and it might be necessary to produce doctor's evidence of suitability to continue riding.
- ☐ A moped entitlement will start at the earliest on the 16th birthday of the holder.
- ☐ A motorcycle entitlement will start at the earliest on the 17th birthday of the holder.
- ☐ The entitlement will last for two years unless the holder passes the D.S.A. Accompanied Rider Test (see conditions of a provisional licence).
- ☐ When the entitlement has been removed from a licence, the holder must wait one year before applying for reinstatement.
- ☐ Car drivers have to undergo the same compulsory basic training as motorcycle riders before the provisional motorcycle entitlement on their licence comes into effect.

TYPES OF MACHINES AVAILABLE

Mopeds

- ☐ A moped is a combination of a low-power motorcycle and a bicycle.
- ☐ Riders may ride a moped unsupervised at 16 years of age on a provisional licence, category P issued after 1 December 1990 only when validated by a CBT certificate. A moped rider with a provisional licence issued before 1 December 1990 may ride on public roads with L-plates for an unlimited period.

- ☐ Anyone who has a full motorcycle licence or a full car licence is qualified to ride a moped on public roads without L-plates, and is able to carry a passenger.
- ☐ A moped rider who has passed the D.S.A. Accompanied Rider Test is exempt from further CBT when applying for a provisional motorcycle entitlement.
- ☐ Mopeds are cheaper and more economical than motorcycles.
- ☐ Moped controls are simple to operate, and many have only a throttle and a front and rear brake. Sports mopeds, which are light-weight motorcycles, have similar controls to a motorcycle.
- ☐ Mopeds have the same handling characteristics as motorcycles with regard to steering, braking, etc.
- ☐ The seat of some mopeds can be adjusted to suit the height of the rider.
- ☐ Mopeds must not be ridden on motorways.

The term 'moped' means a motorcycle which has a maximum speed of 30mph, an engine cylinder capacity (cc) not exceeding 50cc, and an unladen weight not exceeding 250kg. (If the machine was used before 1 August 1977, an engine not exceeding 50cc and pedals which will provide propulsion.)

Scooters

- ☐ Scooters range from those with low powered engines to powerful machines capable of carrying two persons and their luggage for long distances.
- ☐ Riders may ride a scooter exceeding 50cc unsupervised on a provisional licence, category A, at 17 years of age, provided the licence has been validated by a CBT certificate.
- ☐ Provisional licence holders are restricted to scooters

not exceeding 125cc, and subject to the two year motorcycle entitlement.

- ☐ Scooters have small wheels, and need to be steered more than motorcycles, which have larger wheels, and scooters are therefore controlled by balance for much of the time.
- ☐ The engine and transmission of a scooter are situated under the back seat, and the weight carried by the back wheel is greater than that of a motorcycle. This means the proportion of braking done by the rear brake can be increased without affecting the stability of the machine.
- ☐ When securing luggage, avoid loading excessive weight at the rear of the machine. Fix luggage carriers securely in front of or behind the handlebars.
- ☐ Riders must allow for greater stopping distances if carrying extra weight or a passenger, and increase tyre pressures and alter suspension as recommended in the manufacturer's handbook.

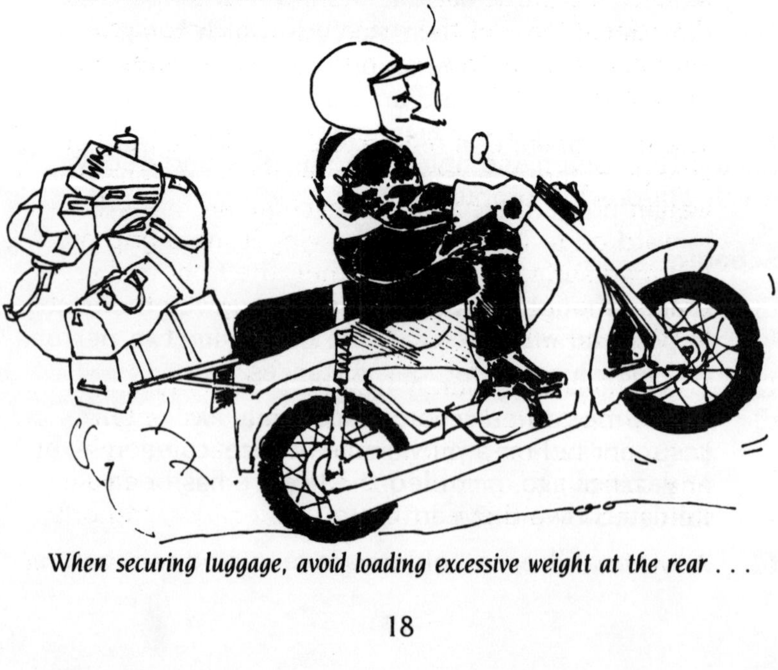

When securing luggage, avoid loading excessive weight at the rear . . .

- ☐ Scooters are less stable than motorcycles on slippery roads.
- ☐ Gears are often operated by the left hand.

Scooters have different handling characteristics to motorcycles because their wheels are smaller and lighter. The engine usually has a cylinder capacity of over 50cc, although some lightweight scooters are within the moped category P. The engine is normally located under the seat.

Motorcycles

- ☐ Riders may ride a motorcycle not exceeding 125cc on a provisional licence, category A, at 17 years of age subject to a two year entitlement, providing the provisional licence has been validated by CBT (see conditions of provisional licence).
- ☐ Motorcycles are 'leaned' rather than steered, except at low speeds or on the open road. The weight of the machine combined with that of the rider, when leaned in a particular direction, will determine the directional force of the machine. The motorcycle automatically centres when the rider assumes an upright position.
- ☐ The front brake of a motorcycle should be applied slightly before the rear brake in dry conditions. The weight of the rider and the machine are then thrown forward on to the front tyre, giving it more grip on the road surface. In wet weather, the front and rear brakes should be applied together, gently to avoid locking the wheels.
- ☐ Loads must be securely fastened. Heavy luggage should be carried in front of the rider using tank bags, not behind, which makes the machine unstable and difficult to control. Use saddle bags for smaller items and avoid overloading panniers or a top box.
- ☐ Allow for increased stopping distances when carrying

extra weight or a passenger, and increase tyre pressures and alter suspension as recommended in the manufacturer's handbook.

There is a wide variety of machines on the market ranging from commuter bikes to sports and trail motorcycles, through to the top high-performance machines.

Motorcycles with sidecars

- ☐ Riders may drive a motorcycle and sidecar on a provisional licence, category A, at 17 years of age subject to the two year motorcycle entitlement, if the provisional licence has been validated by CBT (see conditions and restrictions of provisional licence).
- ☐ The sidecar must travel on the nearside of the motorcycle, i.e. the side nearest the kerb, except for certain imported machines.
- ☐ The motorcycle wheels should be aligned so that when the machine is parked next to the kerb, the front wheel is 1–1½ inches closer to the kerb than the rear wheel. The sidecar wheel must lead the rear wheel, and the motorcycle must lean slightly away from the sidecar.
- ☐ A motorcycle with a sidecar needs to be steered.
- ☐ Motorcycles with sidecars have a tendency to veer to the left while under acceleration. When the driver applies the brakes, the machine will pull to the right. This can be corrected by fitting a sidecar wheel-brake. Skilled riders turn these road-handling characteristics to advantage on a left turn by slowing more than normal, then accelerating round to reduce the risk of the sidecar lifting. Similarly, but depending on the traffic situation, the brakes can be used to aid a right turn.
- ☐ A motorcycle with a sidecar needs a greater distance to stop than a solo motorcycle. Riders may fit a sidecar brake to aid braking, and must apply the

front brake before the rear brake, using greater pressure on the front brake.

Motorcycles with sidecars handle differently to solo motorcycles which are steered largely by balance.

Three-wheeled vehicles

- ☐ Motor-tricycles or three-wheeled vehicles must not exceed 500kg in weight, and drivers may drive them on a provisional licence, category B1, at 17 years of age, or 16 years if receiving a mobility allowance. Learner drivers of category B1 vehicles are not subject to the two year motorcycle entitlement and do not need a CBT certificate but must display L-plates and be supervised by a driver who has held a full licence, category B, for three years and is over 21 years of age.
- ☐ Drivers of three-wheeled vehicles should brake only when the machine is travelling in a straight line.

Motorcycles with sidecars handle differently to solo motorcycles . . .

- ☐ Weight must be distributed evenly around the vehicle, and not to one side.
- ☐ Beware of slippery road conditions.
- ☐ The controls are similar to those of a car.

Three-wheeled vehicles are sometimes made of glass fibre and, due to the uneven weight distribution on the three wheels, and their lightness, can be unstable in high winds, on bends and travelling at speed.

How to choose your machine

Points to consider include:

- ☐ Cost of buying or credit terms.
- ☐ Price of safety equipment and protective clothing.
- ☐ Is the machine taxed? Lower rates are charged for machines under 150cc, higher rates for 150–250cc, and higher still for those over 250cc.
- ☐ Cost of insuring the machine according to the type of cover required. All policies include compulsory passenger cover. Fully comprehensive is the most expensive but insures against all risks. It can pay to 'shop around' several companies or brokers for quotes.
- ☐ Running costs of the machine, including miles per gallon. For example, is the engine a two- or four-stroke engine? Two-stroke is more economical up to 175cc.
- ☐ Maintenance costs vary. Servicing and repairs will be extra expensive if you buy a high mileage second-hand machine. Is the motorcycle three years old or over, and when is the MOT due?
- ☐ How quickly will the machine depreciate, and will the value be maintained when you wish to sell or part-exchange?

- ☐ Are spare parts easily obtainable?

Before buying a moped or motorcycle, check the machine is the right size. Riders should be able to sit astride with both feet flat on the ground and operate all controls comfortably. Ask your local motorcycle dealer or road safety officer about training schemes in your area. Since December 1990, it is an offence for a new learner rider to ride on the road before completing an approved training course for motor vehicles in categories A and P.

Go to a reputable dealer and discuss the availability of different types of machines, your needs, and how much you can afford to pay. Provisional licence holders will not be interested in a 1000cc high-performance motorcycle. Will you be riding short distances, commuting in built-up areas, or travelling up and down hills? Some riders intend travelling a high mileage or carrying heavy loads and need to purchase a machine that fulfils their requirements.

Buying a second-hand machine

- ☐ Ask a qualified mechanic or motoring organisation for a professional opinion before buying privately second-hand.
- ☐ Never buy a second-hand machine without a registration document.
- ☐ Check there are no outstanding hire purchase agreements or loans on the machine.
- ☐ Go to a reputable dealer who can advise you which type of machine is best suited to your pocket and needs.

A second-hand machine will be cheaper than a new one, but there can be pitfalls. An MOT certificate is no guarantee the machine is mechanically sound – only that it was considered safe and complied with certain criteria on the day the machine was examined.

ON THE ROAD

Is your machine legal?

- ☐ Tyres must be inflated to the correct pressure and have at least 1.6mm of tread with no cuts, bulges or bald patches.
- ☐ All fitted lights must be correctly adjusted and work properly.
- ☐ The brakes, steering, speedometer, horn and exhaust system, including the silencer, must be in good working order.

All machines must comply with these legal requirements before being ridden on the road. The above points relate to the condition of the machine, and contribute to the safety of the rider and other road users.

Documents required

- ☐ Current signed driving licence valid for the machine that is being ridden and CBT certificate if applicable for a provisional licence with a moped or motorcycle entitlement.
- ☐ Insurance cover for liability or injury to third parties and passengers. Comprehensive insurance will indemnify damage to the rider's own machine. Motorcyclists should read their policy and schedule. *Some insurance companies have eliminated third party cover when the rider is riding a machine other than their own.*
- ☐ Registration document containing details of the machine and the owner. The appropriate part of the document must be completed and sent to DVLA in Swansea when the machine is sold.
- ☐ A valid tax disc must be displayed on the left-hand side of the machine. This can be purchased from some Post Offices.

- ☐ MOT certificate when a machine is three years old. This can be obtained from an Approved Testing Station and is valid for one year.

2. Equipment and Clothing

SAFETY EQUIPMENT NEEDED

Legal requirements

- ☐ All riders must wear a BSI approved safety helmet securely fastened under the chin.
- ☐ Goggles or visor must be BSI approved.
- ☐ It is an offence to wear a helmet with only a chin cup fastening.

Safety helmets

- ☐ Buy new, BSI approved. Look for the kitemark.
- ☐ Ensure the safety helmet fits snugly and the strap fastens securely under the chin.
- ☐ Choose a white helmet for extra conspicuity, especially at night.
- ☐ Never paint a helmet, add stickers or drill holes in it.
- ☐ Replace your helmet when dropped or damaged. Damage may not be apparent but the helmet could be weakened – perhaps with fatal results.
- ☐ Clean the helmet with warm water and a little soap if really necessary. Do not use petrol-based cleaners, polish, or abrasive creams or pads.
- ☐ Examine the helmet and straps frequently for signs of wear, cracks, damage or fraying.
- ☐ Undo or loosen the chin strap to remove the helmet, and completely fasten the strap before riding any machine.
- ☐ Chin cups should not be used unless there is a second strap fastened under the chin.

There are two types of safety helmets. Open-faced helmets can be used with goggles or a visor. Full-face helmets are fitted with a visor and provide extra protection, but are more expensive. Riders should buy the best quality they can afford, and never purchase a second-hand helmet. A safety helmet should sit firmly on the head and feel comfortable. After fastening the chin strap, use both hands to check the helmet cannot be removed and does not move excessively.

Take care of a safety helmet. Never hang it up by the strap, or place it upside down on a flat surface. Both these practices can weaken the structure. Remember that in the event of an accident, the safety helmet may have to protect your head from sudden impact with the road!

Visors and goggles

- ☐ Visors and goggles must be BSI approved. This will ensure they have an anti-scratch coating of the highest quality.
- ☐ Choose a visor that can be raised easily by hands when wearing leather gloves, and locks down when required.
- ☐ Replace scratched goggles or visors immediately.
- ☐ Avoid scratching the surface with fine grit, and keep a soft clean cloth to wipe the surface gently.
- ☐ Choose a visor or goggles with clear glass. Tinted glass can reduce visibility at night, in bad weather, or where light is reduced on shady roads or in tunnels.

Good eye protection is vitally important for the safety of the motorcyclist. Eyes are extremely fragile, and irreplaceable. They are vulnerable to wind, rain, dust, grit, flies and other insects. Spray and mud thrown up from vehicles in bad weather conditions are additional hazards. Draughts and wind make eyes water and reduce visibility.

Goggles and visors should be non-splinter and shatter-proof giving a wide range of vision. Ensure they fit comfortably, and replace straps as soon as they begin to fray or sag. Damaged eyes could mean damaged eysight – forever. Intelligent riders protect their eyes from injury.

Glasses

- ☐ Glasses or goggles used under a visor must fit properly.

The same rules about tinted glass apply. Keep a clear pair of glasses, with thin rims and frames to aid peripheral vision, for riding. Riders who prefer tinted lenses, thick rims, or heavyweight plastic frames must carry a second pair for motorcycling which give good front and side vision. Keep glasses clean, and have a spare pair in case of breakage or loss.

Photochromic lenses do not work well inside a visor. All riders should have their eyes examined by a qualified optician every two years unless recommended otherwise. Riders can ask their optician for a prescription lens for goggles.

SUITABLE CLOTHING

General rules

- ☐ Clothing should fit without flapping or riding up and exposing the body.
- ☐ Specially designed clothing will have room underneath for other garments.
- ☐ Be seen and buy bright clothing, especially over-garments such as waterproof clothing.

Clothing should be warm, comfortable and fit properly. Choose a strong material which will protect your skin if you fall off a moped or motorcycle. Leather and denim are ideal, and waxed cotton and some nylon suits with double-strength seams have good 'slide' properties on abrasive surfaces.

Gloves

- ☐ Choose leather gloves whenever possible.
- ☐ Use waterproof overmitts during rain.
- ☐ Stick or sew reflective material on gloves.

Ensure gloves fit properly and are not stiff and heavy. Wear a pair of cotton gloves under normal gloves in cold weather for extra warmth. Some gloves are now fitted with a small 'wiper blade' on the thumbs and this is ideal for clearing the visor in wet weather conditions. Always wear gloves; riders instinctively use their hands during a fall and this can result in serious injuries to unprotected hands, especially on tarmac.

Clothing should fit without flapping . . .

Jackets

- ☐ Buy bright waterproof jackets to prevent other clothing becoming wet during rain or mist.
- ☐ Padding on shoulders and elbows provides extra protection.
- ☐ Fluorescent or reflective vests, sashes and belts should be worn over dark jackets at night.

Light-weight jackets allow the arms to bend comfortably. Jackets should be hip length, and should not ride up to expose the motorcyclist's back. The sleeves must cover the wrists.

Trousers

- ☐ Trousers should fit comfortably and not be tight.
- ☐ The ends of trousers must be tucked into boots to prevent turn-ups flapping and catching on the machine.

Trousers should be of a strong material, ideally leather. In the event of an accident, legs may become trapped or broken. Strong trousers can provide some protection.

Footwear

- ☐ N*ever* wear wellington boots or trainers.
- ☐ Do not allow laces to dangle. Tie them securely.

Buy strong boots that cover the calf. If shoes are used, they should protect the ankle. Allow room for two pairs of socks in cold weather. Special overboots for wet weather can be purchased.

Waterproof clothing

- ☐ Buy waterproof clothing which is light and comfortable.

- ☐ Wear bright colours to enable other road users to see you in poor weather conditions.

Waterproof clothing should fit over protective clothing without restricting the rider or flapping about.

Remember, a warm dry rider is a safer rider!

3. Maintenance and Safety

KEEPING A MACHINE IN A ROADWORTHY CONDITION

The condition of a machine will affect its performance, reliability, handling characteristics and, above all, the safety of the rider. It is essential that mopeds, scooters and motorcycles are properly maintained. This applies to all machines, and especially ones which have a high mileage or were purchased second-hand. Owners should read the maker's instruction book and follow the recommendations given with regard to service intervals and maintenance.

Cleaning and polishing

- ☐ Wash the machine with clean, warm water.
- ☐ Wash paintwork, lights, reflectors and number plates.
- ☐ Try to prevent electrical parts becoming wet.
- ☐ Paintwork and chrome may be polished, *but do not polish parts you hold or operate*, for example, the seat, brake pedals, foot rests, etc. This could make them slippery, and therefore dangerous.
- ☐ Keep polish away from brakes, discs and pads which could become contaminated and reduce the effectiveness of the brakes.

Conscientious riders take pride in the appearance of their machines. By keeping a machine clean and tidy, riders are able to see which parts are lost, damaged, or need replacing. Washing and polishing the chrome and paintwork prevents corrosion in the winter when salt deposits accumulate, and will increase the resale value.

Daily Safety Checks

Riders should have a working knowledge of their machines and motorcycle training schemes include basic maintenance in their syllabus. Spend a few minutes each day *before* riding your machine to make the following checks. A word of warning – all checks should be in addition to routine servicing and maintenance, not instead of it.

☐ *Fuel.* Check for leaks. Visually check the fuel level.

☐ *Oil.* Check the oil level on flat ground.

☐ *Lights.* All lights must be clean, working properly, and correctly adjusted.

☐ *Brakes.* Check the stopping power of the front and rear brakes. Examine the brake cables, particularly at the nipple ends, for signs of fraying or wear. Check the brake fluid level in machines with hydraulic brakes.

☐ *Tyres.* Visually check tyres for signs of damage, and ensure that the tread depth is well within legal requirements, or the braking distance and stability can be seriously reduced. Use a reliable tyre pressure gauge to make sure the pressures comply with the manufacturer's manual. To obtain accurate figures check the tyres when cold. Reduced pressure gives advance warning of tyre damage. Beware when gauges have both metric and imperial measurements, and use the correct one.

☐ *Steering.* Check for excessive movement in head bearings by grasping fork ends firmly and trying to move them backwards and forwards.

☐ *Suspension.* Push down on the machine to check the suspension is working properly.

☐ *Chains.* Check the chain has the correct amount of free play by turning the wheel until the chain is fully stretched. Adjust until the up and down movement at the half-way point is that recommended in the maker's instruction manual.

☐ *Cables*. Check the brake, clutch, and throttle cables are not frayed or worn, especially at the nipple ends, to prevent cable failure.

☐ *Mirrors*. Adjust and clean the rear view mirrors.

☐ *Tool kit*. Carry a basic tool kit and spares. Include bulbs, spare spark plug, fuses, a tyre valve core, and a plug spanner.

Weekly checks

☐ *Leaks*. Check carefully for oil or fuel leaks.

☐ *Chain*. Check for wear in the chain or sprocket and replace if necessary. The closed end of the spring link must face in the direction the chain rotates. Keep the chain clean and oiled. It is dangerous to allow the chain to become loose, but beware of overtightening. See the owner's manual for adjustment details.

☐ *Brakes*. Check pads and shoes for wear. Adjust brake cables if needed. Lubricate brake cables taking care not to contaminate brake pads.

☐ *Tyres*. Check valve caps are fitted to all valves, and the fitting line is parallel to the rim on both sides of each tyre. Remove objects such as stones from the tread.

☐ *Battery*. Top up the battery with distilled water, and grease the terminals to prevent corrosion. Make sure the breather pipe is clear.

☐ *Clutch*. Check the clutch cable for wear, and ensure there is the correct amount of free play in the lever. Lubricate the cable according to the manufacturer's handbook.

- ☐ *Steering*. Check the wheel alignment using a straight line or a piece of wood. To check the wheel bearings, grasp the wheel firmly in both hands and try to twist it for excessive sideways movement.
- ☐ *Ignition*. Check the spark plugs have the correct gap and are in good condition. Replace plugs that have a white deposit or appear oily, but use the type recommended in the manufacturer's handbook.
- ☐ *Lubrication*. Use the correct grade of oil and change at the recommended intervals. Lubricate the gearbox when necessary, and the cables and chain as mentioned.
- ☐ *Nuts and bolts*. Check nuts, bolts, circlips and split pins. Tighten, adjust or replace as necessary.

Correct and early diagnosis of potentially serious faults can save money, and enable the fault to be repaired before the machine becomes a danger either to the rider or other road users. Riders with some mechanical knowledge will be able to see whether repairs requested have been completed.

Do not attempt to undertake repairs which are better left to professional mechanics. This is a false economy and an unsafe practice. When in doubt, ask a reputable motorcycle dealer for advice. The weekly check on your machine should incorporate the daily checks, but be more thorough and include the above points.

Adjusting a machine to individual requirements

- ☐ *Seating*. Riders should be able to sit astride their machines with both feet flat on the ground. Some seats are adjustable.
- ☐ *Hand operated controls*. Handlebars should be adjusted so the handgrips are level or sloping downwards.
- ☐ *Footrests*. Footrests should be adjusted for easy access to the brake pedal, and the brake pedal adjusted to

assist this action. Legs should be bent at the knees and the feet resting comfortably on the footrests.

Experienced motorcyclists know that the ability to control a machine is reliant on a comfortable seating position. Riders must be able to reach and operate all the controls in a relaxed manner without having to stretch. Every second may be vital in an emergency.

BE SAFE - BE SEEN

Why motorcyclists are vulnerable

Motorcycles are a third of the width of a car and more easily missed when:

- ☐ Visibility is poor.
- ☐ The motorcyclist is hidden from view by lamp posts, parked cars, or other obstructions.
- ☐ The motorist has sub-standard vision or poor observation.
- ☐ The rider is wearing dark clothing which merges with the background.

Two out of three accidents occur at road junctions. Many drivers involved in these accidents state they 'did not see the motorcyclist approaching'.

How to be seen

- ☐ Check lights are clean and working.
- ☐ Use dipped headlights during the day time, and not only during poor visibility.
- ☐ Keep a good separation distance from other vehicles.
- ☐ Wear a white safety helmet.
- ☐ Wear bright clothing and a fluorescent vest over a jacket.
- ☐ Stick or sew reflective flashes on gloves and clothing.

The above practical advice is no substitute for careful and courteous riding, but will increase a rider's safety on the road. All motorcyclists must make themselves and their machines as conspicuous as possible. Following the above advice could save lives. Many of these points have been mentioned already, but are so important they cannot be over-emphasised.

4. Motorcycle Training

COMPULSORY BASIC TRAINING (CBT)

- ☐ Compulsory basic training replaced Part 1 of the Motorcycle Test in December 1990.
- ☐ Training does not have to be completed in one day.
- ☐ The provisional moped or motorcycle entitlement is not valid until the rider has undergone compulsory training and has obtained a CBT certificate.
- ☐ At the end of the compulsory basic training course the rider will be issued with a 'Certificate of Completion of an Approved Training Course for Motor Vehicles in Categories A and P' (see pages 40–41) which will validate the motorcycle or moped entitlement on the provisional licence.
- ☐ Organisations, training bodies and dealers approved by the D.S.A. will be responsible for basic training and the issue of certificates to riders who have successfully completed the course.

About the certificate

- ☐ The certificate of completion of training has to be earned. A trainee can only progress from one objective of the basic training course to the next when the instructor is satisfied they are ready.
- ☐ Before issuing a certificate of completion of training, the instructor must ensure the learner rider has the ability to control the motorcycle or moped; can manoeuvre the machine competently; and is safe to ride on the road unsupervised.
- ☐ The certificate must be signed by the successful candidate in the presence of the instructor.
- ☐ The certificate will validate the provisional licence

entitlement and allow the holder to ride unaccompanied (but displaying L-plates) on the road.

- ☐ The certificate must be sent to the regional office of the D.S.A. together with a D.S.A. test application form when the holder applies to take the Motorcycle Accompanied Rider Test, or the certificate must be shown to the examiner together with the provisional licence immediately before the test.
- ☐ In the event of loss, a duplicate certificate can be obtained from the training body who issued the original. *This certificate is an official document – take care of it.*

Types of training schemes

- ☐ The aim of basic training is to ensure new riders are safe on the road and fully aware of a rider's responsibilities as a road user.
- ☐ Riders may choose from schemes which are split into sessions, or are completed in one day.
- ☐ Training organisations may supply tuition machines because it is illegal for trainees to ride their machines on the road until the basic training course is completed.
- ☐ A learner who wishes to use their own motorcycle or moped must make arrangements for the machine's delivery to the training ground or off-the-road facilities provided.
- ☐ During training, riders should have the opportunity to respond to instructions and directions given over a voice-activated radio by an accompanying rider, and received via an earpiece, in preparation for the Accompanied Rider Test.
- ☐ At the end of the course, the instructor must be satisfied that the learner rider has the ability to control the motorcycle and can manoeuvre it competently before issuing the validation certificate.

DRIVING STANDARDS AGENCY

Road Traffic Act 1988

Certificate of Completion of an Approved Training Course for Motor Vehicles in Categories A and P

Driver Number of Candidate

Hrs Mins

Date and time of course completion

Current name

Current address

Postcode

has successfully completed an approved training course for motor vehicles in categories A and P, prescribed for the purpose of Section 97 of the Road Traffic Act 1988 as amended by Section 6 of the Road Traffic (Driver Licensing and Information Systems) Act 1989.

Signature of Instructor — appointed to conduct such training

Initials and Surname (BLOCK CAPITALS) — No.

The successful candidate should sign in ink below in the presence of the instructor.

Signature

Official Stamp of Training Body — Site at which Course conducted and Site No.

DL 196

An Executive Agency of the Department of Transport

Certificate of Completion DL196 – *front*

Important

This certificate is **NOT** a licence to drive, but will validate your provisional licence entitlement to drive a motorbicycle as a learner driver (ie unaccompanied and displaying 'L' plates). You must keep this Certificate with your provisional licence at all times.

You must produce this Certificate to the Examiner when attending for your driving test (unless you have produced it with your application for the appointment for the test) otherwise the test will be terminated and your fee will be forfeit.

Notes:

1 Make sure you keep a separate note of the date and place where you completed your course. If you lose this form a duplicate may be obtainable from the training body with whom you took the course.

2 This Certificate **DOES NOT** exempt you from any requirements to display 'L' plates, nor does it permit you to carry on a solo motor bicycle any passenger.

3 This Certificate is valid for 3 years. It will validate a provisional licence for both categories A (motorcycle) and P (moped).

Certificate of Completion DL196 – *reverse*

Contents of an approved training course

Module one – Introduction
Trainees must be told and understand:

- ☐ The aims of the approved training course.
- ☐ The importance of having the right equipment and clothing.
- ☐ The need to be clearly visible to other road users (the use of conspicuity aids).
- ☐ The legal requirements for riding on the road.
- ☐ Why motorcyclists are more vulnerable than most road users.
- ☐ The need to ride at the correct speed according to road and traffic conditions.
- ☐ The importance of reading and understanding the Highway Code.

Trainees' eyesight must be tested. Trainees must be able to read in good daylight a vehicle registration mark containing letters and figures 79.4mm high at a distance of 20.5 metres (with the aid of glasses or contact lenses if required).

Module two – Practical on-site training
Trainees must receive practical on-site training which enables them to:

- ☐ Become familiar with the motorcycle, the controls and how it works.
- ☐ Be able to carry out basic machine checks and be able to take the bike on and off the stand.
- ☐ Wheel the machine around to the left and right showing proper balance, and bring the motorcycle to a halt by braking.
- ☐ Start and stop the engine satisfactorily.

Module three – Practical on-site riding

- ☐ Ride the machine under control in a straight line and bring the machine to a controlled halt.
- ☐ Ride the machine round a figure of eight circuit.
- ☐ Ride the machine slowly under control.
- ☐ Bring the machine to a stop under full control as in an emergency.
- ☐ Carry out controlled braking using both brakes.
- ☐ Change gear satisfactorily.
- ☐ Carry out rear observation correctly.
- ☐ Carry out simulated left and right turns correctly using the Observation-Signal-Manoeuvre (OSM) and Position-Speed-Look (PSL) routines.

Module four – Practical on-road training
Before undertaking practical on-road training, trainees must be told and must understand the need to:

- ☐ Ride defensively and anticipate the actions of other road users.
- ☐ Use rear observation at appropriate times.
- ☐ Assume the correct road position when riding.
- ☐ Leave sufficient space when following another vehicle.
- ☐ Pay due regard to the effect of varying weather conditions when riding.
- ☐ Be aware of the various types of road surfaces that can be encountered.

Module five – Practical on-road riding
Trainees must ride safely in a variety of situations, including as many of the following as possible:

- ☐ Roundabouts.
- ☐ Junctions.
- ☐ Pedestrian crossings.
- ☐ Traffic lights.
- ☐ Gradients.
- ☐ Bends
- ☐ Obstructions.

Trainees must undertake on-road riding under the supervision of a D.S.A. Certified Instructor. Certified Instructors are the holders of a CBT1, a yellow certificate which contains a photograph of the instructor and must be carried during courses.

Trainee records

Detailed records must be kept to record the progress of each trainee. On pages 46 and 47 is an example of the way the five modules of an Approved Training Course will be recorded by the training scheme.

Is further training necessary?

- ☐ After completing a CBT course, a rider has up to two years in which to pass the D.S.A. Accompanied Rider Test, or else lose the provisional motorcycle or moped entitlement for one year (see conditions of provisional licence).
- ☐ On completion of CBT, learner riders will be able to ride their machines unsupervised on the road.
- ☐ Further training using radio controlled equipment will give the learner rider the opportunity to practice correct road procedures and gain experience safely in a variety of traffic conditions.
- ☐ Further training will prepare provisional licence holders for the standard of riding required by the

D.S.A. in order to pass the Accompanied Rider Test before the provisional licence entitlement expires.

- ☐ The learner rider must be able to respond to instructions and directions given over a voice-activated radio by an accompanying rider or driver, and received via an earpiece.

ROSS-ON-WYE RIDER TRAINING SCHEME	TRAINEE RECORD
NAME	
ADDRESS	
POSTCODE	

Motorcycle	Reg. No.	Tel. No. (Home) (Work)	Receipt No.

Driver No.	Insurance Expiry	MOT Expiry	Date of Training

MODULE 1 Safety and Legal Requirements			
Aims of Basic Training		Legal requirements, eg Ins.	
Clothing and Helmets		Motorcycle Vulnerability	
Conspicuity		Speed	
Eyesight		Routine Maint (Theory)	
MODULE 2 Practical On-Site Training			
Routine Maint (Practical)		Using brakes with Dead Engine Pushing Machine L/R	
Intro to Controls		Turning L/R with Dead Engine Pushing using Brakes	
On and Off Stands		Starting and Stopping Engine	
MODULE 3 Practical On-Site Riding			
Clutch Control		Dangers of Over Braking (Theory)	
Riding in a Straight Line		Controlled Stop	
Walkabout		Rear Observation	
Slalom		Signals	
Figure of Eight		Left and Right Turns	
Changing Gear		Emergency Stop	

Training scheme record – side one

MODULE 4 Practical On-Road Riding			
Rear Observation		Parked Cars	
Road Position		Hill Start, Up and Down	
Left Turn		Pedestrian Crossings	
Right Turn		Traffic Lights	
Defensive Riding		Roundabouts	
Braking Gap		Road and Weather Conditions	
MODULE 5 Conclusion			
Drink & Drugs		Accident Risk	
Care, Courtesy and Consideration		Importance of Certificate	
Importance of Further Training			
Record of Certificate			
Certificate No.			
Issued By			
Centre M.M.T.A. ROSS-ON-WYE. MERCN/003			
Date		Time	

TRAINEE TO READ THESE NOTES CAREFULLY AND SIGN BELOW BEFORE ANY TRAINING IS STARTED

1a) If you are using your own machine it must be taxed, insured, and have an MOT certificate if more than three years old.

1b) If you have not attained the required standard at the end of the training session you will be responsible for removing your machine from the site. Remember you must not ride it on the road until you have a Certificate of Completion of Basic Training.

2) You must provide an approved safety helmet that fits you, together with strong gloves and suitable footwear.

I have read and understood the above notes.

Signed Date

Training scheme record – side two

5. The D.S.A. Accompanied Rider Test

ABOUT THE MOTORCYCLE TEST

There are a variety of 'tall tales' circulated by riders who have failed their motorcycle test – and sometimes by those who passed! Everybody has heard some of these stories. The facts are, D.S.A. motorcycle examiners are highly skilled and experienced motorcyclists. All are specially selected and have undergone intensive training and testing at the Examiner's Establishment at Cardington in Bedfordshire, to prepare them for the rigorous requirements of the accompanied motorcycle test.

Routes are standardised as far as possible, and designed to incorporate a variety of traffic conditions and different junctions over a distance of eight to ten miles. Whether a motorcyclist takes the test in Monmouth or London, the D.S.A. tries to ensure all learner motorcyclists receive a similar and fair test of their riding ability.

Some riders may claim to have failed from 'nerves'. However, learners on test normally ride at a higher standard when nervous. The stress causes adrenalin to flow which heightens awareness and anticipation. Riders whose nerves let them down must learn to ride safely whatever the conditions. Ignore tall stories: the job of a driving examiner is to pass safe riders. If you ride safely and competently on your test, you will pass.

How the examiner conducts the motorcycle test

In October 1989, the D.S.A. Accompanied Rider Test replaced the Part 2 Motorcycle Test.

Examiners use a standard wording, and directions are clear and concise. At the start of the test in the Test Centre, the examiner says "Good morning Mr Jones" or "Good afternoon Miss Smith", as appropriate. The candidate must sign the examiner's sheet and produce their driving licence. The following is then asked: "Will you lead the way to your machine please?"

After the eyesight test, the examiner walks round the candidate's machine to check there is no damage to indicators or lights. Regulation L-plates must be clearly displayed front and rear, and the machine should be roadworthy with no unauthorised modifications.

During the test, the examiner gives directions by a voice-activated radio, and riders are supplied with a radio receiver to enable them to hear the examiner when 'on the move'. It may be necessary for the examiner to use a car to follow the candidate but this is still expected to represent a proper test of the rider's ability. Before the test begins, the rider is told to stop if a loss of radio contact occurs. In this event the equipment is checked before the test resumes.

The start of your test

The examiner will tell you to follow the road ahead unless traffic signs direct otherwise, or instructions to the contrary are received. The examiner will give an example of the type of message, for example, "Take the next road on the left" or "Pull up along here by the lampost". It will be explained that in the event of you and the examiner becoming separated, perhaps by traffic lights, it may be necessary to ask you to pull up on the left and wait for a few moments.

All the directions are clear and given in good time. The examiner will follow by motorcycle or car, and the test starts when you both leave the D.S.A. Test Centre. Fairly early in the test, the examiner will direct you to ride to a specially designated area where the manoeuvres are conducted. The examiner will dismount to conduct the emergency stop, angle start and U-turn manoeuvres, and when these are completed the examiner will get back on the motorcycle or into the car and continue the accompanied part of the motorcycle test.

Test routes cover about 10 miles and take approximately 35 minutes. The examiner may ask you to ride as if in slow moving traffic for a short distance towards the end of the test if these skills have not been required in normal traffic situations. Non-English speaking candidates will be followed by the examiner and an interpreter, who is supplied by the candidate, in a car. Deaf candidates will be given the opportunity to learn the test route, and will be asked to stop at pre-arranged places during the test.

Time passes quickly and at the end of the test the examiner asks questions on the Highway Code and other motoring matters relevant to learner riders, and shows pictures of road signs to be identified. Successful candidates are told "That is the end of your test and I am pleased to tell you, you have passed." However, if a candidate has failed, "That is the end of your test. I am sorry you have not passed but your riding has not reached the required standard. If you will give me a few moments, I will help you by marking the points to which you should give special attention." The examiner will complete the relevant forms and return to the Test Centre.

How the Motorcycle Accompanied Rider Test is marked

The examiner is trained to watch the riding of a test candidate and assess what are serious and dangerous faults. Riders are not judged on their appearance, or how many passes or failures the examiner has 'notched up' the previous week. Each test is marked individually.

Mistakes made by a rider during the Accompanied Rider Test are marked by the examiner on the examiner's Driving Test Report. Serious faults are marked with an X, and dangerous faults when others are forced to take action or are exposed to unacceptable risk, are marked with a D, and a candidate will fail if one or more serious or dangerous faults are committed. The faults marked on the examiner's Driving Test Report are underlined on the Statement of Failure which is given to the candidate, and each fault is shown in one section only.

DRIVING STANDARDS AGENCY
'Safe driving for life'

Driving Test Report

DL 25 (Rev 10/90)

Centre

Date / /

Candidate's full name

Name of School (where known)

Particulars of vehicle P C S

Make

Type

Group

Reg Mark

Year 19

FET		1
HC		2
PRE		3
ACC		4
CL		4
G		4
F.BR		4
H.BR		4
ST		4
MO PRE		5
CON		5
ES		6
FR.BR		6
RV CON		7
OBS		7
TR CON		8
OBS		8

MIR	SIG		9
	DIR		9
	ST		9
ROB	SIG		9
	DIR		9
	ST		9
SIG	O		10
	W		10
	L		10
SNS	ST		11
	DIR		11
	NE		11
	RM		11
TRA	L		11
	CON		11
SIG	ORU		11
PRO	+		12
PRO	–		13

J	SP+		14
	OBS		14
	POSR		14
	POSL		14
	RCC		14
OT			15
MAT			15
CAT			15
POSN			16
SH.V			17
PX			18
NS			19
AA	PED		20
	CYC		20
	DRI		20
ETA	V		
	P		

Driving Test Report DL25 – *front*

Weather Conditions	Route Number
Brief description of candidate	
Remarks	
D 10 No	Examiner's Signature
DL 24 No	

Disability Tests - Including eyesight failures

Driver Number	
Description of any adaption fitted	

Driving Test Report DL25 – *reverse*

DRIVING STANDARDS AGENCY

Statement of Failure

Road Traffic Act 1988

00

An Executive Agency of the Department of Transport

Name [ ] Test Centre [ ]

has this day been examined and has failed to pass the test of competence to drive prescribed for the purposes of Section 89 of the Road Traffic Act 1988.

Date [ ]

Authorised by the Secretary of State to conduct tests.

Examiners have regard to the items listed below in deciding whether a candidate is competent to drive. The matters needing special attention are marked for your information and assistance and should be studied in detail. (see Note 1 overleaf)

1 ☐ Comply with the requirements of the eyesight test.

2 ☐ Know the Highway Code.

3 ☐ Take proper precautions before starting the engine.

4 ☐ Make proper use of accelerator, clutch, gears, footbrake, steering, handbrake.

5 ☐ Move away safely, under control.

6 ☐ Stop the vehicle in an emergency promptly, under control, making proper use of front brake.

7 ☐ Reverse into a limited opening either to the right or left under control, with due regard for other road users.

8 ☐ Turn round by means of forward and reverse gears under control, with due regard for other road users.

9 ☐ Reverse park under control, with due regard for other road users.

10 ☐ Make effective use of mirror(s), take effective rear observations well before signalling, changing direction, slowing down or stopping.

11 ☐ Give signals where necessary, correctly, in good time.

12 ☐ Take prompt and appropriate action on all traffic signs, road markings, traffic lights, signals given by traffic controllers, other road users.

13 ☐ Exercise proper care in the use of speed.

14 ☐ Make progress by driving at a speed appropriate to the road and traffic conditions, avoiding undue hesitancy.

15 ☐ Act properly at road junctions:-
- -regulate speed correctly on approach;
- -take effective observation before emerging;
- -position the vehicle correctly before turning right, before turning left;
- -avoid cutting right hand corners.

16 ☐ Overtake, meet, cross path of, other vehicles safely.

17 ☐ Position the vehicle correctly during normal driving.

18 ☐ Allow adequate clearance to stationary vehicles.

19 ☐ Take appropriate action at pedestrian crossings.

20 ☐ Select a safe position for normal stops.

21 ☐ Show awareness and anticipation of the actions of pedestrians, cyclists, drivers.

Driving Examiners are NOT permitted to discuss details of the test **DL 24 (Rev 01/91)**

Statement of Failure DL24 – *front*

Guidance Notes

1. More detailed advice about the test requirements and the items marked for your attention overleaf are given in the Driving Standards Agency's book "Your Driving Test". This book, published by HMSO (obtainable from bookshops) also contains the "Recommended Syllabus for Learning to Drive".
2. You should not only make a study of the book but ensure that you achieve basic competence in all aspects of the "Syllabus" before you take your next test.
3. The Department's manual "Driving" (obtainable from bookshops) and a study of the relevant rules in the Highway Code, will also be of help to you.
4. No further tests on a vehicle of the same Category can be undertaken until the expiry of one calendar month.
5. If you lose this form a duplicate may be obtained from the Driving Standards Agency, Regional Office.

Appeals

5. If you consider that your test was not properly conducted in accordance with the Regulations you may apply to a Court of Summary Jurisdiction acting for the Petty Sessional Division in which you reside (in Scotland to the Sheriff within whose jurisdiction you reside) which has the power to determine this point. If the Court find that the test was not properly conducted they may order a refund of the fee and authorise you to undergo a further test forthwith. (See Road Traffic Act 1988, Section 90).
6. You should note, however, that your right to apply to the Court under section 90 is strictly limited to the question of whether the test was properly conducted in accordance with the Regulations. **In particular the Court cannot question the merits of the examiner's decision.**

Statement of* Failure DL24 – *reverse

The result of the D.S.A. Accompanied Rider Test

At the end of the motorcycle test, candidates who pass receive a pass certificate from the examiner. This must be forwarded to DVLA together with the provisional driving licence, or full licence for other groups, and a completed driving licence application form.

When a candidate is given a Statement of Failure (DL24), the examiner will explain briefly why the points are listed, but this is discretionary and will only take place if the candidate is receptive. Mistakes made during the test will not be discussed in any detail and the decision of the examiner is final. A candidate may appeal only if the test was not conducted within the requirements of the 1988 Road Traffic Act, for example if the examiner failed to carry out the emergency stop exercise or an angle start or any other legal requirement. An appeal, if upheld, would result in a retest being offered.

The sample sheets reproduced on the next three pages illustrate how a D.S.A. examiner would mark the following faults committed by a candidate who has failed: 'Signals given too late to warn other traffic of an intended manoeuvre' and 'Turning right in front of oncoming traffic and causing another driver to brake'.

DRIVING STANDARDS AGENCY

'Safe driving for life'

Driving Test Report

DL 25 (Rev 10/90)

Centre: MONMOUTH

Date: 16/01/91

Candidate's full name: TOM JONES

Name of School (where known): —

SPECIMEN

Particulars of vehicle	P C S	Make	HONDA
		Type	NSR 125
Group	A	Reg Mark	H123 ABC
		Year	1990

FET			1
HC			2
PRE			3
ACC			4
CL			4
G			4
F.BR			4
H.BR			4
ST			4
MO	PRE		5
	CON		5
ES			6
	FR.BR		6
RV	CON		7
	OBS		7
TR	CON		8
	OBS		8

MIR	SIG		9
	DIR		9
	ST		9
ROB	SIG		9
	DIR		9
	ST		9
SIG	O		10
	W		10
	L	X	10
SNS	ST		11
	DIR		11
	NE		11
	RM		11
TRA	L		11
	CON		11
SIG	ORU		11
PRO	+		12
PRO	–		13

J	SP+		14
	OBS		14
	POSR		14
	POSL		14
	RCC		14
OT			15
MAT			15
CAT		D	15
POSN			16
SH.V			17
PX			18
NS			19
AA	PED		20
	CYC		20
	DRI		20
ETA	V		
	P		

Example of completed Driving Test Report – front

Weather Conditions	Route Number
DRY SUNNY	1

Brief description of candidate

FAIR, MEDIUM HEIGHT / BROWN LEATHER JACKET
WHITE HELMET & VISOR.

Remarks

Candidate signalled late before turning left into Hamlet St

Candidate signalled late before turning right into the High Street.

Candidate turned right at at the junction of High Street with Bank Rd infront of a white van which braked sharply.

D 10 No	Examiner's Signature
DL 24 No	[signature]

Disability Tests - Including eyesight failures

Driver Number	J O N E S 5 1 1 1 1 7 0 T J 9 R U

Description of any adaption fitted

NONE

Example** of **completed** Driving Test Report – **reverse

DRIVING STANDARDS AGENCY

Statement of Failure

Road Traffic Act 1988

An Executive Agency of the Department of Transport

00 SPECIMEN

Name TOM JONES Test Centre MONMOUTH

has this day been examined and has failed to pass the test of competence to drive prescribed for the purposes of Section 89 of the Road Traffic Act 1988.

Date 16/01/91

Authorised by the Secretary of State to conduct tests.

Examiners have regard to the items listed below in deciding whether a candidate is competent to drive. The matters needing special attention are marked for your information and assistance and should be studied in detail. (see Note 1 overleaf)

1 [ ] Comply with the requirements of the eyesight test.

2 [ ] Know the Highway Code.

3 [ ] Take proper precautions before starting the engine.

4 [ ] Make proper use of accelerator, clutch, gears, footbrake, steering, handbrake.

5 [ ] Move away safely, under control.

6 [ ] Stop the vehicle in an emergency promptly, under control, making proper use of front brake.

7 [ ] Reverse into a limited opening either to the right or left under control, with due regard for other road users.

8 [ ] Turn round by means of forward and reverse gears under control, with due regard for other road users.

9 [ ] Reverse park under control, with due regard for other road users.

10 [ ] Make effective use of mirror(s), take effective rear observations well before signalling, changing direction, slowing down or stopping.

11 [X] Give signals where necessary, correctly, in good time.

12 [ ] Take prompt and appropriate action on all traffic signs, road markings, traffic lights, signals given by traffic controllers, other road users.

13 [ ] Exercise proper care in the use of speed.

14 [ ] Make progress by driving at a speed appropriate to the road and traffic conditions, avoiding undue hesitancy.

15 [ ] Act properly at road junctions:-
-regulate speed correctly on approach;
-take effective observation before emerging;
-position the vehicle correctly before turning right, before turning left;
-avoid cutting right hand corners.

16 [X] Overtake, meet, cross path of, other vehicles safely.

17 [ ] Position the vehicle correctly during normal driving.

18 [ ] Allow adequate clearance to stationary vehicles.

19 [ ] Take appropriate action at pedestrian crossings.

20 [ ] Select a safe position for normal stops.

21 [ ] Show awareness and anticipation of the actions of pedestrians, cyclists, drivers.

Driving Examiners are NOT permitted to discuss details of the test **DL 24 (Rev 01/91)**

Example of completed Statement of Failure

REQUIREMENTS OF THE D.S.A. MOTORCYCLE ACCOMPANIED RIDER TEST

1. The eyesight test

Before the motorcycle test, the examiner will ask you to read a vehicle registration plate containing letters and figures 79.4mm high at a distance of 20.5 metres (with the aid of glasses or contact lenses if needed), in good daylight.

It is a legal requirement to be able to read a number plate at this distance before driving or riding a vehicle and if difficulty is experienced the examiner will measure the distance exactly. For your own safety, have your eyesight checked regularly by a qualified optician.

2. The Highway Code

You will be asked questions on the Highway Code and other motoring matters, and you will be asked to identify six road signs and markings at the end of the test. Prepare for this part of the test using the 'Driving Test Questions and Answers' book referred to in the foreword. The following twenty questions are a sample of the type of questions that could be asked to test your knowledge of safe riding practices. The answers to these questions can be found in the book referred to.

Sample questions for riders

1. Why is it important to maintain correct tyre pressures?
2. What parts of a motorcycle should be adjusted to suit the individual rider?
3. How should a pillion passenger sit on the machine?
4. Is a pillion passenger required to wear a protective helmet?
5. What problems can carrying a pillion passenger cause, particularly when cornering?

6. What dangers can arise from wearing defective goggles or visors?
7. Why should centre and side stands be fully raised before moving off?
8. What problems could arise from not fully raising the centre and side stands before moving off?
9. What changes in the road surface should a motorcyclist look for?
10. Describe the types of road surface that can cause problems for the motorcyclist?
11. Why is it important for a motorcyclist to watch out for manhole covers?
12. What precautions would you take when riding in wet conditions after a long dry period?
13. What dangers can arise for a motorcyclist as a result of fuel spillage from other vehicles?
14. What are the dangers of not wearing a visor or goggles when riding?
15. Why should a motorcyclist who is riding for a reasonable distance wear the right type of clothing?
16. What is the importance of a correct and comfortable riding position?
17. Why could it be difficult for a motorcyclist to be seen in traffic?
18. What precautions can motorcyclists take to make themselves or their machines more conspicuous to other road users?
19. Why is it important when braking firmly for the machine to be upright and travelling in a straight line?
20. How would you apply the brakes when stopping in an emergency?

3. Checks before starting the engine

- ☐ *Safety helmet.* Put on your helmet and fasten the strap. This will be done with the examiner after the installation of the ear pieces.
- ☐ *Radio link.* A radio receiver will be fastened round the waist. The examiner will check the operation of the radio by means of a test message.
- ☐ *Eyes.* Pull down visor or fasten goggles.
- ☐ *Gloves.* Put on your gloves.
- ☐ *Fuel.* Check there is sufficient fuel and switch on the petrol switch.
- ☐ *Stands.* Check the stands are fully raised.
- ☐ Switch ignition on.
- ☐ Check the machine is in neutral *before* starting the engine. (If the engine stalls, check again before switching on.)
- ☐ Use left leg to support the machine.
- ☐ Turn the throttle and start the machine. (Use choke in cold weather and no throttle until the engine is warm.)

4. Using the controls

Throttle

The throttle is hand-controlled and usually situated on the right-hand side of the machine. It should be operated smoothly and progressively. Using the throttle harshly, then having to brake sharply, is not good motorcycle practice and wastes fuel. Revving the engine when the machine is stationary can cause damage and premature wear and also annoy local residents. Release the throttle and make use of engine braking before applying front and rear brakes. This will be more effective in a four-stroke engine.

Clutch

The clutch lever is operated by all four fingers of the left hand. Use the clutch when moving off, changing gear, for slow manoeuvring, and stopping. Before moving off, hold the clutch at biting point. This is the point of contact between the engine and the back wheel, and you can feel and hear when this point is reached. To move forward, turn the throttle and gradually increase the revs. The secret of smooth starting lies in the skillful co-ordination of the clutch and throttle.

Using the clutch to maintain control when manoeuvring at low speeds is called clutch control. Do not use the clutch unnecessarily or the machine will coast (freewheel) and be more difficult to control. Coasting is marked as a gears fault.

Gears

Gears are usually operated by the left foot, and the rider should not look down before changing gear. Change gear when travelling in a straight line, and co-ordinate the use of the clutch, throttle, and gears. Choose the correct gear for the speed the machine is travelling, the gradient of the road and the relevant traffic conditions.

Speed up before changing up, one gear at a time, and gently rev the throttle to enable a smooth gear change to be made. Plan ahead and reduce speed by first easing off the throttle, then braking before selecting the correct gear and changing down. Increase the throttle sufficiently, prior to releasing the clutch, to effect a smooth change. It is not essential to change down one gear at a time.

Before coming to a standstill, change down in the gears so that, in the event of a change of situation ahead, you are ready to ride on immediately without impeding the progress of following traffic, especially on a hill start exercise. Select neutral when stationary for more than a few seconds, for example while waiting at red traffic lights.

Common faults include riding for too long in low gears, and not changing down in the gears early enough when speed has been reduced. Do not coast by operating the clutch lever between gear changes as this can cause a potentially serious loss of control.

Front and rear brakes
The front brake is usually controlled by the right hand and is operated by all four fingers. The important rule is to apply the front brake fractionally before the rear brake. This throws the weight of the machine forward on to the front tyre, and gives greater adhesion and grip on the road surface. The rear brake should then be applied to complete the slowing down process, thereby giving maximum stability to the machine. Riders who use only the rear brake lose this benefit, and the back wheel will tend to slide.

In dry weather, the proportion of front to back brake being applied should be 75/25 respectively. In wet weather, the proportion of front and rear brakes being applied should be 50/50, but the front brake should still be operated first. The rear brake is normally controlled by the right foot.

The brakes should be operated smoothly and progressively using the observe - signal - lifesaver routine. Riders must plan ahead and brake gently in wet weather conditions, or when the machine is travelling at speed, to avoid locking the wheels. (See Emergency Stop below for the safe procedure to follow in the event of this happening.)

In order to reduce the risk of skidding, riders should slow when the machine is upright and being ridden in a straight line, not when entering bends or turning right or left, and not on white paint or drain covers, etc. Allowance should be made for the brake light to give adequate warning of an intended manoeuvre.

Steering
The centre of the handlebar grips must be held lightly but firmly with wrists naturally down. A good riding

position is elbows slightly bent, shoulders relaxed, hips neither too far forward nor too far back. Riders are advised to grip the petrol tank with their knees to aid balance, and not lean forward excessively. Avoid jerky movements and looking down at the controls or switches, such as lights, choke, etc. All steering movements must be smooth, balanced and well-planned.

Riders must observe well ahead, and be aware of their whole field of vision without fixing their eyes on any one spot. Slowing before bends, and slightly increasing speed out of them, ensures maximum control. The back wheel takes a short cut when the machine turns a corner and turning too early results in the machine hitting the kerb or cutting a corner. Both are dangerous practices.

You must be able to balance your machine and ride under control at low speeds and, in the latter stages of the test, the examiner may ask you to ride for 20–30 yards as if in slow moving traffic, if you have not had to ride slowly in the various traffic situations already encountered during the test.

5. Moving off

A motorcyclist should be able to move off smoothly whatever the gradient, ahead and at an angle, and without endangering other road users. The angle start exercise (moving out from behind a parked vehicle), is performed in the early stages of the test. The examiner will give the instruction: "Ride on when you are ready, please".

Safely

Before moving off, use the following routine:

- ☐ O*bserve*. Look behind and around.
- ☐ S*ignal*. Signal if necessary to warn other road users.
- ☐ L*ifesaver*. Look behind and around again and, if clear,
- ☐ M*anoeuvre*. Move off if safe, and give way to pedestrians who may be crossing the road.

Under control
To move off smoothly:

☐ Decrease throttle, disengage clutch and depress gear shift pedal to select first (low) gear.

☐ Release clutch lever to biting point.

☐ Co-ordinate throttle and clutch lever to move off smoothly.

☐ Both feet should be on the footrests as the machine starts to move forward. Slowly increase throttle as required.

To start the machine on a hill repeat the procedure, except

☐ Hold the front brake before starting the engine.

☐ After selecting first gear, change to foot-operated rear brake.

☐ Co-ordinate the rear brake, clutch and throttle to prevent the machine rolling or stalling when moving off.

6. Emergency stop

Many test candidates are nervous of the emergency stop exercise. At the beginning of the motorcycle test, the examiner directs the candidate to a specially designated area before dismounting and explaining the exercise, including a demonstration of the stop signal. The candidate is then directed to ride round a block until the examiner gives the rider the stop signal. The examiner should be standing ahead of the candidate about two feet into the road and in full view. The examiner will not suddenly appear from behind a tree.

When the examiner gives the signal to stop, the rider is expected to stop the machine under full control, making proper use of the front brake. The U-turn exercise and angle start may be conducted at the same location.

The examiner will not suddenly appear from behind a tree.

Promptly
Candidates must obey the examiner's instructions and, when the signal to stop is given, react quickly and stop safely. This is an emergency stop and it is not necessary to look behind before stopping.

Under control
Riders should hold the handlebars firmly and operate the front brake fractionally before the rear brake. If the rear wheel locks, the rear brake should be released until the wheel is turning again, and then reapplied more gently. Leave the clutch alone until the machine has almost stopped and, when stopped, put the machine into neutral.

After the emergency stop exercise has been completed, the test will continue with the examiner following the candidate and giving directions.

7. Reversing exercise

This does not apply to motorcycles and mopeds.

8. Turning in the road (U-turn)

After the emergency stop exercise, the examiner will ask the rider to perform a U-turn to demonstrate balance and control at low speeds. The examiner will say "I'd like you to ride along this road for a short distance and, when convenient, turn round and come back to stop on the opposite side." ('By means of forward and reverse gears' will be deleted on the DL24.)

Under control
Keep the machine under control by co-ordinating the use of the clutch, throttle and brakes. Candidates should try to keep their feet off the ground but will not necessarily fail if this is not possible.

Observation
Check the road is clear before beginning the U-turn and do not forget the vital lifesaver look. To continue the test in the original direction, the examiner will ask you to push or ride the machine across the road.

9. Reverse park

This does not apply to motorcycles and mopeds.

10. Using the mirrors/rear observation

It is important to be aware of following traffic, especially before a manoeuvre. Using mirrors or glancing round is not enough. Riders must look properly over the shoulder in order to assess the traffic situation behind them, but not for too long or steering and forward vision will be affected. Whether a machine has mirrors is immaterial. All riders must remember the lifesaver look. It is essential to check behind in good time before making any riding decisions, and observation must be effective.

Before signalling
Riders must know how their signals will affect other road

users, and look over the shoulder well before giving signals either by arm or indicator, to check the position of following traffic. Decide whether a signal, and what type of signal, is necessary and when to give it.

Before changing direction
It is important to check behind before turning left or right, overtaking moving or parked vehicles, moving into another lane, or any other change of direction. Never forget the lifesaver look before any manoeuvre.

Before slowing or stopping
All riders must observe behind before slowing or stopping, except in an emergency when there is not time. The speed and distance of following traffic affects the rate at which riders can reduce speed safely.

11. Giving signals

Signals are necessary to help or warn other road users. Since the examiner follows the candidate round the test route, signals are required before all manoeuvres on test.

Signals are necessary to help or warn other road users.

Correctly
Only indicator or arm signals in the Highway Code should be used, and the indicators should be cancelled when a manoeuvre is completed. If they self-cancel too early, they should be switched on again. A slowing down arm signal, not a turning left signal, should be given when the rider is pulling up. Riders must not flash the headlight at other drivers, and not beckon to drivers or pedestrians to cross the road, possibly into danger from other road users.

In good time
Signals are intended to warn other road users in good time of an intended riding action. It can be misleading to signal too early, especially where junctions are close together.

12. Acting on signs and signals

Traffic signs
Learn the meanings of the different traffic signs as given in the Highway Code. All riders must act correctly on the warning or order given.

Road markings
Road markings give riders valuable information regarding road junctions, hazards and positioning. Some roads are marked with arrows to help riders and drivers choose the correct lane, or to give advance warning of deceleration lanes. Try to avoid braking on road markings because the wheels will not grip the white paint. Riders should avoid the metal studs on the approach to junctions for the same reason.

Traffic lights
Red, red and amber, and amber traffic lights mean stop, except in the case of amber if riders have already crossed the line, or are so close to it that to stop would cause an accident. Green traffic lights mean go *if* the way is clear, and riders are expected to check before riding on. Traffic

lights can change quickly, and temporary traffic lights may be partially obscured by vehicles or road works.

Signals given by traffic controllers
Signals given by police officers, traffic wardens, and school crossing patrols showing a 'Stop – Children' sign must be obeyed. It is an offence, and dangerous, to ignore them.

Other road users
Riders must watch for signals given by others, and use good judgement and common sense to assess situations, then act promptly. Never rely on others, and be extra careful where people are in charge of animals such as horses or cattle.

13. Care in the use of speed

Observe speed limits. Candidates who show disregard for legal limits will not pass the motorcycle test. It is not always safe to keep up to limits. Ride at a speed at which it is possible to stop safely should the need arise. When roads are wet, riders should allow at least twice the normal distance to stop a machine safely. Traffic conditions, the road surface, pedestrians and animals must be considered when deciding the speed at which to travel. The examiner will not expect you to ride at a speed greater than that dictated by the prevailing traffic conditions.

14. Making progress

In present day traffic conditions, it is important not to impede the flow of traffic. Keep up to speed limits where conditions are favourable. Riding too slowly can inconvenience other road users, causing them to become impatient and commit driving errors, such as unplanned overtaking.

Avoiding undue hesitancy
Riders who fail under this section sometimes confuse

being extra careful with hesitancy. Undue hesitancy is being indecisive to a degree which could endanger or inconvenience other road users. Do not wait at 'Give Way' junctions when it is safe to ride on. Stopping for no reason, or acting in a hesitant manner, can be marked as faults by the examiner. Candidates who stop needlessly when it is safe to proceed will fail as, by this misjudgement of the traffic situation, the rider will have shown their riding has not reached the standard needed to pass the D.S.A. Accompanied Rider Test.

15. Road junctions (including roundabouts)

Regulate speed correctly on approach

On the approach to a road junction, a rider must allow sufficient time to follow the observe-signal-lifesaver routine and the position-speed-look routine. Candidates should slow to a safe speed before selecting the correct gear. At 'Stop' junctions, stop prior to emerging but, at 'Give Way' junctions, only stop if the way is not clear to go or vision to the road being entered is limited by an obstruction, for example a lorry parked on a corner.

Riding too slowly can inconvenience other road users . . .

Take effective observation before emerging

This is the section usually referred to when failed candidates complain they *only* failed on observation. Before emerging from a junction, all riders and drivers should use the look-assess-decide routine.

LOOK from a position where visibility is good. When the view is restricted, perhaps by parked vehicles or pedestrians, edge slowly forward looking right and left until it is possible to see both ways. ASSESS the situation carefully. DECIDE whether it is safe to go.

Decisions fall into one of three categories: safe; unsafe; or unsure. When it is safe, emerge promptly and, if unsafe, wait until the traffic clears. Riders who are unsure whether it is safe to ride on should treat the situation as unsafe and wait or edge forward if an obstruction blocks the view.

Not all learners have enough riding experience on which to base decisions, and some riders emerge before the correct decision has been made. Look carefully before moving into or crossing any junction, whether it is your priority or not, and watch for other motorcycles or cyclists.

Position the vehicle correctly before turning right

Riders should follow the routines described in the section on effective observation. Generally, riders turning right should move just left of the centre of the road, and wait at the point of turn for oncoming traffic to pass safely. Do not obstruct the path of other vehicles. The exceptions to this rule of positioning are narrow roads where riders must keep left to allow room for vehicles turning in, and one way streets and dual carriageways where the right-hand lane should be used. Remember the lifesaver look before turning.

Position the vehicle correctly before turning left

Keep reasonably to the left when turning left and do not swing out thus endangering other road users. Use deceleration lanes to slow down. Remember the lifesaver look, and watch for cyclists alongside before turning the machine.

Avoid cutting right-hand corners
Riders turning right should not lean or steer too early. Cutting the corner of a road junction places the motorcyclist on the wrong side of the road being entered, and unable to see approaching traffic. This is a dangerous practice and would be marked as a serious fault.

16. Overtaking, meeting and crossing the path of other vehicles

Overtake other vehicles safely
Overtaking is a dangerous manoeuvre. Do not overtake unless really necessary and make sure the manoeuvre can be completed safely on a suitable stretch of road. The road ahead should be clear of hazards. Look behind to ensure it is safe to begin the manoeuvre. Before overtaking, use the position-speed-look routine and then the observe-signal-lifesaver routine. Repeat as necessary.

Never squeeze a motorcycle between two vehicles.

Select the correct gear to provide the power needed, and move out. Never squeeze a motorcycle between two vehicles. Allow a good clearance between your machine and the one being overtaken, and check by looking over your left shoulder that it is safe before moving back into the left-hand lane. Do not cut in on the vehicle you have overtaken. Allow cyclists sufficient room to ensure that there would be no danger from your machine if they were to wobble or fall. The Highway Code details places where overtaking is prohibited or inadvisable.

If in doubt - DON'T. *Overtakers get to the undertakers quicker!*

Meet other vehicles safely
Some roads narrow unexpectedly. Parked vehicles and road works have the same effect on wider roads. Watch for places where there is not enough room to meet oncoming traffic safely. If in doubt, wait back and let approaching traffic pass before driving on. Never squeeze through narrow gaps.

Cross the path of other vehicles safely
Riders turning right and crossing the path of oncoming traffic must wait and give way if their machine would cause other drivers to slow, swerve or stop. All road users should keep a special watch for motorcyclists or cyclists who may be difficult to see. Misjudging the speed or distance of approaching traffic can be dangerous, especially when riding a motorcycle, which is not seen as easily as a wider vehicle.

17. Position on the road

At the beginning of the test, the examiner will instruct the test candidate to: "Follow the road ahead unless traffic signs direct otherwise, or unless I direct you to turn, which I will do in good time. Move off when you are ready, please."

Test candidates must follow the road ahead at crossroads,

staggered junctions and roundabouts, if no other direction is given. Keep to the left of the road unless a manoeuvre requires moving to the right, for example, to overtake or turn right at a road junction.

Riders should avoid riding near the gutter where road debris collects. Drains and potholes are other common hazards. Riders should also not ride too near the middle of the road, causing an obstruction to other vehicles.

18. Passing stationary vehicles

When passing stationary vehicles, divide the maneouvre into three parts and follow a generous safety line.

- ☐ *The approach*. Look ahead and decide if there is room to pass safely. Do not attempt to squeeze past parked cars when there is oncoming traffic. If in doubt, wait well back.
- ☐ *Passing*. Do not shave the corner of stationary vehicles and allow good clearance in case a door opens, the vehicle moves off, or a child runs out.
- ☐ *Pulling in*. Wait until it is safe to move back into the left-hand lane.

19. At pedestrian crossings

Pedestrians using a pedestrian crossing have right of way, and riders must stop and wait until pedestrians have been allowed precedence. When there is a central refuge, treat both sides as a separate crossing. If people are waiting to cross, it is courteous and safe to stop and wait. A slowing-down arm signal should be given to warn others you intend to slow or stop and this will be expected on the test.

Riders should never beckon pedestrians to cross. They could be directing them into danger from other vehicles. It is an offence to park within the zig-zag lines on the approach to a pedestrian or pelican crossing.

At a pelican crossing, pedestrians have right of way when the red light shows to traffic and when amber lights are flashing to allow them to finish crossing safely. Riders may go if the crossing is clear when the amber light is flashing. A pelican crossing that is staggered on each side of a central refuge should be treated as two separate crossings.

20. Selecting a safe position for normal stops

Sometimes an examiner will specify the place a test candidate should stop, for example: "Will you pull up along here by the brick wall, please." Other times the examiner may say: "Pull up on the left at a convenient place, please."

Choose a place that is safe, legal and convenient. The Highway Code gives details of places to avoid. Stop close to the kerb and parallel to it.

21. Awareness and anticipation

Look ahead and anticipate the actions of other road users as soon as is practical. The examiner is watching for quick reactions, not decisions made at the last moment due to lack of forethought and observation. Expect the unexpected and take the appropriate action when it occurs.

Pedestrians
Pedestrians may step out suddenly, especially those walking on the road. Allow plenty of clearance, slow down and be ready to stop if necessary. The old may not see or hear you, and young children are often unpredictable. Give way to pedestrians crossing at road junctions and look out for people with white sticks or guide dogs.

Cyclists
Take extra care when cyclists are about. Watch for them at all times, especially in slow moving traffic, or when you

are crossing lanes used by cyclists. Wait back until it is safe to pass and allow enough clearance to anticipate the possibility that the cyclist could wobble or fall.

Drivers

Be aware of drivers and other motorcyclists when approaching junctions, where the road narrows, or near pedestrian crossings where traffic may slow or stop quickly.

Try to keep a safe distance between your machine and other traffic. Not all drivers and riders are experienced. Do not be surprised if another road user does something stupid. Anticipate the error and act promptly.

6. A-Z of Safe Riding Skills and Techniques

Congratulations, you have passed your riding test. This means you have taken the first steps to becoming a good rider but there are many riding skills to learn as you gain experience. Responsibility for others should be your most important consideration when using the roads. A moment of carelessness or lack of concentration can have tragic results, and pedestrians, cyclists and motorcyclists are particularly vulnerable.

Now that you have passed your motorcycle test, you can use motorways but first make sure you are comfortable riding at higher speeds and that you understand motorway signs and regulations. If you are keen to develop your riding skills, contact your local Road Safety Officer for details of advanced courses offered by I.A.M. and R.O.S.P.A. It takes time, effort and responsibility to become a good rider. Aim to get there safely.

Accident procedure

At the scene of an accident

- ☐ STOP in a safe place.
- ☐ Your machine should not cause an obstruction.
- ☐ Allow plenty of room for emergency services if needed.

Warning other traffic

- ☐ Warn traffic quickly without endangering yourself.
- ☐ Put out cigarettes or naked lights.
- ☐ Switch off the engines of machines or vehicles involved in the accident.

After collision, fire is the main danger, especially where petrol has been spilled.

Warn traffic quickly without endangering yourself.

Alerting the emergency services

- ☐ Dial 999 and state which services you require.
- ☐ On a motorway, use the nearest emergency telephone.
- ☐ State the location, type of vehicles involved and number of casualties.

Whoever contacts the emergency services must give clear and accurate details. If an accident involves a vehicle displaying hazard information panels, ensure the emergency services are given all the available details. Some goods, for example poisonous gases and radioactive loads, require full protective clothing to be worn, so *keep well back*.

Dealing with casualties

- ☐ Do *not move casualties* unless in obvious danger.
- ☐ Do not remove a motorcyclist's safety helmet.
- ☐ Keep people warm and reassured.
- ☐ Apply first aid if necessary.
- ☐ Give *nothing* to eat or drink.

People who are injured are more likely to go into shock when moved or cold. Use blankets, coats or jackets to keep casualties warm, and talk quietly giving reassurance until an ambulance arrives.

Serious internal injuries may not be immediately apparent, and moving a casualty who has spinal or neck injuries can result in paralysis or death. Never attempt to take off the safety helmet of a motorcyclist, as this may aggravate head or neck injuries. Only consider moving an injured person if another life-threatening danger, such as fire, presents a serious risk.

First aid

- ☐ Carry a first aid kit on your machine.
- ☐ Learn first aid. St. Johns Ambulance, St. Andrews Ambulance and the British Red Cross run first aid courses.

The life-saving first aid which may be needed at road traffic accidents while waiting for the emergency services to arrive principally concerns breathing and bleeding.

If breathing has stopped

- ☐ The throat of the injured person should be clear of tongue, false teeth, etc.
- ☐ Support neck and tilt head back.
- ☐ If breathing does not restart, hold nostrils shut and blow into the mouth every four seconds. Watch the

chest rise and fall. Stop when breathing starts.

How to stop heavy bleeding

- ☐ Apply firm pressure to the wound using a clean cloth.
- ☐ If glass or other sharp material is in the wound, apply pressure to a pressure point before the wound.
- ☐ Raise unbroken arms or legs to lessen bleeding.

Procedure for those involved

- ☐ Stop as soon as possible.
- ☐ Give your name, address and motorcycle registration number to those involved.
- ☐ Give the owner's name and address if different from your own. If you are unable to do so, report the accident to the police within 24 hours and produce your insurance certificate at the same time or within 7 days at any Police Station.
- ☐ The accident must be reported to the police within 24 hours if another person is injured or if someone else's property has been damaged.
- ☐ You must provide details of your insurance to any person who has reasonable grounds for wanting to see it.

When you are involved in a road traffic accident these rules should be followed if there is injury to anybody, or damage to other vehicles or property, including fences, street lights and road signs. The police may want to see other driving documents.

Information needed

- ☐ Names and addresses of other riders and drivers involved.
- ☐ Details of other machines and vehicles involved.

- ☐ Insurance details of other riders and drivers.
- ☐ Names and addresses of passengers and witnesses.
- ☐ Make a plan or sketch showing the position of vehicles.
- ☐ Note the time and exact location of the accident.
- ☐ Write down the names and identification numbers of the police who attend the accident and anything another driver, rider or witness says. Read notes back to confirm they are accurate and keep them to produce in court if needed.

Do not admit liability, or say anything that could be used against you at a later stage such as "I am sorry". Note any name or address which could prove useful, and also jot down registration numbers of vehicles parked in the vicinity. The owners can be traced later if necessary. As soon as practical, write a full account of what has happened, and make a sketch showing the position of other vehicles or machines. It may be useful to carry a camera and take a photograph.

Leaving the scene

Wait until the emergency services arrive before leaving the scene of the accident. Even if your vehicle was not involved, the police may wish to question you. Do not allow casualties to wander off: they could be concussed or in shock.

Insurance claim against another rider or driver

- ☐ Contact your insurance company and ask for the relevant claim form.
- ☐ Complete the form and return it promptly.
- ☐ State clearly if you wish your claim to be made against the insurance company of another driver or rider.
- ☐ Do not allow any damage to your machine to be

repaired until the insurance company's assessor has inspected it.

- ☐ Claims for expenses should be made direct to the other insurance company as soon as practical.

Keep a claim form at home and complete it in pencil first in case of errors. Bonuses are awarded for 'no claims', not 'no blames'. Liability must be proved before an insurance company will pay out. If delays occur, ring the company and take the name of the person you deal with. Ask for the claim to be attended to promptly.

Expenses for damaged clothing, any excess you may have to pay, etc. should be claimed directly from the other insurance company. Send your claim together with relevant receipts. When large amounts are involved, seek advice from a solicitor.

Motorcyclists should read their policy *and* schedule. Some insurance companies have eliminated third party cover when the rider is riding another machine.

Bends

Approaching a bend

- ☐ Slow down, taking particular account of weather and road conditions.
- ☐ Select the correct gear before entering a bend.
- ☐ Hold a steady position.
- ☐ Maintain a steady speed to round a bend.

The correct speed will depend on visibility, the camber of the road, whether the surface is wet or dry, the angle of the bend, etc. Speed should be at its lowest the moment you begin to steer into a corner. Being in the right gear and using gentle acceleration to round a bend will increase the stability of the machine. Your chosen speed should reflect the possiblity of unexpected hazards, or errors made by other road users.

Leaving a bend

- ☐ Gently accelerate when leaving a bend.

Distractions

The rider

- ☐ Looking down at the controls.
- ☐ Wiping visor or goggles.

Concentrate on 'reading the road ahead' at all times and do not look down to operate any of the controls or switches, for example, gears or lights.

Other distractions

- ☐ Friends or relatives on the pavement.
- ☐ Beautiful scenery.
- ☐ Hot air balloons or planes taking off from an airport.
- ☐ Direction signs.
- ☐ Shop windows.

Other distractions . . .

The list is endless, with different riders being distracted in a variety of ways. Losing concentration can be fatal for a rider, especially when riding at speed or at night.

Eyesight

General rules

- ☐ Glasses should have thin rims and frames.
- ☐ Do not wear tinted glasses or photochromic lenses under goggles.
- ☐ Replace a scratched visor or goggles immediately.

Riders must be able to read, in good daylight, a vehicle registration plate at a distance of 20.5 metres, with glasses or contact lenses if needed. Avoid yellow tinted glasses which make it difficult to see cyclists, parked cars and pedestrians in the shadows. The same applies to blue tinted glass where there is sodium lighting. Riders are advised to have their eyes tested every two years and some optometrists now have equipment capable of measuring a rider's field of vision.

Fitness to ride

Riders must not ride if:

- ☐ Eyesight is defective and uncorrected.
- ☐ A relevant disability is present.
- ☐ Under the influence of alcohol.
- ☐ Under the influence of drugs.
- ☐ Tired or unwell.

Licence holders must notify DVLA when a relevant disability is present, for example, attacks of epilepsy.

Never drink and ride. Decisions, reaction time, judgement and balance can be seriously impaired even below the legal limit of 35 microgrammes of alcohol per 100 millilitres of breath. Many drugs which can be bought over the counter and are in common use can affect riders. Examples are cough mixtures, cold and flu preparations, and hay fever remedies. If in doubt, always check with a pharmacist.

When riders are unwell or tired, their reactions are slow. Never drive or ride unless you are in good health and feeling fit.

Flood water

When riding through water:

- ☐ Check the depth of the water, using roadside points of level when possible.
- ☐ Use a low gear.
- ☐ Slip the clutch and keep the engine speed high.
- ☐ Maintain a slow steady speed.

Use your common sense before making a decision whether to ride through flood water. Ride at a low speed and avoid making waves which could cause your machine to break down. After riding through water check brakes are working properly. If not, dry them out by gently applying the front hand-controlled brake but check that it is safe to do so.

Check the depth of the water . . .

Fog code

- ☐ Check your mirrors and reduce speed so you can stop safely within your range of vision.
- ☐ Be seen. Switch on a dipped headlight.
- ☐ Speed is deceptive in fog. Allow for unexpected hazards.
- ☐ Watch for parked vehicles, cyclists and pedestrians.
- ☐ Obey any special speed limits, especially on motorways. Observe all warning signals.
- ☐ Allow more time for your journey.

Take extra care when it is foggy, especially when the fog is patchy or drifting; or when riding in fog after dark.

Rules for following other drivers

- ☐ Following closely behind another vehicle's tail lights gives a false sense of security.
- ☐ Do not keep up with vehicles in front unless they are travelling at a safe speed.
- ☐ If another vehicle is following too closely behind your machine, do not increase speed. Pull up if necessary and let the vehicle pass.

Hanging on to tail lights can be dangerous. If the vehicle in front disappears from view, it may be because the fog has thickened, rather than the vehicle has increased speed. If there is an obstruction ahead, the vehicle in front may stop quickly. Leave enough room to be able to stop safely and under control. Larger vehicles travelling ahead will be displacing thick fog and making conditions seem clearer than they are. D*o not ride in fog unless your journey is absolutely necessary and allow more time.*

Lights which should be used

- ☐ Switch on dipped headlight.

It is important to see and be seen in fog. Keep lights, indicators and reflectors clean of grime and moisture. Beware of other vehicles, especially lorries, whose rear lights may be obscured by dirt thrown up from the road. Park off the road in foggy conditions.

Headlights

When to use the main beam headlight

- ☐ At night.
- ☐ Out of 30mph zones where there is no street lighting.
- ☐ When you are not following traffic and there are no oncoming vehicles.

Make yourself visible to others by riding with a dipped headlight during the daytime. When riding on main beam, dip the headlight when following other vehicles, or oncoming traffic approaches.

Horn

Correct use of the horn

- ☐ The horn should not be used when your machine is stationary, unless to avoid an accident.
- ☐ The horn must not be used on a moving vehicle between 11.30pm and 7.00am in a built up area.
- ☐ Use as a warning and do not sound for longer than necessary.

The horn should only be sounded as a timely warning and should say "Look I am here" and not "Get out of my way". A short, sharp toot is often sufficient to let others know you are there. Use the horn when about to overtake another vehicle whose driver may be unaware of your presence; approaching sharp bends in country lanes; to alert playing children; or when you anticipate another driver or rider may cause a collision.

Junction procedure

Approaching a road junction

- ☐ Look well ahead and note road signs and lane markings.
- ☐ Follow the observe-signal-lifesaver-manoeuvre routine.
- ☐ Position the machine correctly, keeping in the left-hand lane when going straight ahead in the absence of signs or markings to the contrary.
- ☐ Slow down as necessary, then select the correct gear.
- ☐ Watch carefully for obstructions, pedestrians, motorcycles and cyclists.
- ☐ Stop at 'Stop' junctions, when necessary at traffic lights and for pedestrians crossing the road.

Emerging from a road junction

- ☐ Ensure you can see clearly both ways.
- ☐ Assess the situation.
- ☐ Decide whether it is safe to proceed.

It may be necessary to edge out slowly into the junction when there are parked cars or other hazards blocking the view. Do not emerge until it is safe. A high proportion of accidents happen to vehicles and machines turning right. Take care before crossing the path of other traffic, and never cut right-hand corners as this can cause a collision (see page 73). Remember the lifesaver look before turning.

Check both ways before riding past or emerging from any junction, whether or not it is your priority. The art of safe riding is not only to avoid causing accidents but to avoid being the victim of another road user's carelessness.

Roundabout procedure
The following is the correct signalling and positioning:

- ☐ *Turning left.* Signal left and approach in left-hand lane.
- ☐ *Straight ahead.* Do not signal. Keep in left-hand lane unless road markings or signs instruct otherwise.
- ☐ *Turning right.* Signal right and approach in right-hand lane.
- ☐ When your machine has passed the exit before the one you wish to take, signal left to notify others of your intention to leave the roundabout.

Roundabouts are junctions where fast-moving traffic merges, and it is necessary to judge the distance and speed of approaching vehicles accurately. Follow the observe-signal-lifesaver-manoeuvre routine and give way to traffic from the immediate right unless road markings indicate otherwise.

Keep in the right-hand lane when turning right at a roundabout, and check exit roads as you pass. Remember the lifesaver look over the left shoulder before signalling left and leave the roundabout in the left-hand lane, unless it is obstructed by slow-moving traffic. Avoid articulated lorries as the trailer may take a short cut. Riders should take care not to become trapped in a lorry's manoeuvring space or sandwiched between vehicles.

Beware of other road users who do not signal or position their vehicles correctly and of drivers who may not have seen you.

Crossroads procedure

- ☐ Approach as for other junctions.
- ☐ Obey traffic light signals.
- ☐ Look both ways before proceeding and give way if it

is not safe to cross the junction, even if it is your priority.

- ☐ When turning right, pass offside to offside if possible but nearside to nearside at staggered junctions or where road or traffic conditions dictate.

Turning right at crossroads can be a hazardous manoeuvre for a rider. Other drivers may not see you. Look for hazards and be ready to stop if necessary.

Traffic lights

- ☐ Red means stop.
- ☐ Amber means stop.
- ☐ Green means go *only* if the way is clear.

When the traffic lights are amber, keep going if you have crossed the stop line, or are so close to it that to stop would cause an accident. Check the way is clear before riding on, and anticipate the lights may change or pedestrians cross the road. Be prepared to give way.

Loads

- ☐ All loads must be secure.
- ☐ Spread the weight of loads evenly.
- ☐ Loads must not affect visibility or obscure lights.

It is an offence to ride with an unsafe load. Avoid carrying excessive weight at the rear of your machine. Securely fasten luggage. Check headlight alignment and increase tyre pressures and suspension as recommended by the manufacturer.

Mirrors

- ☐ Ensure mirrors are clean.
- ☐ Adjust the mirrors correctly before riding your machine.

- ☐ Mirrors have blind spots and it is important to check over your shoulder before any manoeuvre. Remember the lifesaver look.

Good rear observation is vital. Use the mirrors and look over your shoulders. Never forget the lifesaver look.

Motorway riding

Preparation for a motorway journey

- ☐ Do not travel if you are tired or unwell.
- ☐ Your motorcycle must be in good mechanical condition.
- ☐ Check tyres for damage, wear and correct pressures.
- ☐ Ensure fuel, oil and coolant levels are adequate for your journey.

Do not travel if you are tired . . .

- ☐ Study an up-to-date map and note your junction exit numbers.
- ☐ Plan regular stops for refreshment and rest at service areas.

Mopeds, and learner drivers on motorcycles are not allowed on motorways. Motorways are designed to be safe. There are no roundabouts, crossroads, sharp bends, pedestrians or slow-moving traffic. Vehicles travelling on a motorway are driven at high speeds on carriageways of two or more lanes. Lane discipline and adequate separation distances are extremely important.

Riders travelling long distances at high speeds must remember to inflate their tyres according to the manufacturer's handbook.

Manoeuvres prohibited on motorways

- ☐ Stopping, unless in an emergency or in service areas.
- ☐ U-turns.
- ☐ Crossing the central reservation.
- ☐ Riding against the traffic.

Motorway information signs

Illustrations of these can be found in the Highway Code. They comprise:

- ☐ Advance warning signs of a motorway.
- ☐ Start of a motorway.
- ☐ Motorway interchanges.
- ☐ Service areas.
- ☐ Direction of nearest emergency telephone.
- ☐ Motorway exit signs at approximately 1 and ½ mile.
- ☐ Route confirmation signs after an exit.

- ☐ Countdown markers to a deceleration lane at 300, 200, and 100 yards.
- ☐ Distance to next two service areas.
- ☐ Local radio information signs for traffic news.
- ☐ End of motorway signs.

Joining a motorway

- ☐ Motorways often start at a roundabout.
- ☐ Blue rectangular signs give advance warning.
- ☐ Use the slip road and acceleration lane if provided.

The slip road joining a motorway leads to an acceleration lane. Use this lane to adjust your speed to that of the traffic already on the motorway. Enter the left hand lane of the motorway when a suitable gap appears. When the motorway is busy, you may have to wait in the acceleration lane. Never force traffic to slow or swerve.

Motorway lights and studs

- ☐ Amber flashing lights mean hazard ahead. Reduce speed to under 30mph.
- ☐ Red flashing light means STOP. Do not go any further in that lane.
- ☐ Amber studs mark the right-hand edge of the carriageway.
- ☐ Red studs mark the left-hand edge of the carriageway.
- ☐ Green studs separate the acceleration and deceleration lanes from the carriageway.

Flashing lights may warn of dangers ahead such as fog or accident. The lights will flash at intervals on the motorway. Some amber lights have an illuminated sign giving advance warning of a lane closure, temporary advisory speed limits, or the end of a previous restriction. Some signs warn of a particular hazard, for example, fog.

If red lights flash on a slip road, it means you must not enter it. The coloured studs on the carriageway are helpful at night and when visibility is poor, by marking the edges of the carriageways.

Riding on a motoway

- ☐ Ride in the left-hand lane unless overtaking.
- ☐ Ride in the middle of the lane.
- ☐ Use dipped headlights.
- ☐ Leave an adequate separation distance between yourself and other vehicles.
- ☐ Use rear observation constantly to monitor changing traffic situations.
- ☐ Do not forget the lifesaver look before all manoeuvres.

Leave a gap of *at least* one metre per mph of your speed, or follow the two-second rule and leave a two-second gap between your machine and the vehicle in front. Measure two seconds by repeating the phrase 'Only a fool breaks the two second rule'. In bad weather conditions a longer gap must be left.

Avoid riding two abreast and do not get boxed in. Always look for an 'escape' route. Heavy goods vehicles and vehicles towing trailers are not allowed to use the third, right-hand, lane of the motorway. Beware, bridge supports and long vehicles which have broken down will act as temporary windbreaks. These can cause a rider to lose balance in windy conditions.

Overtaking on motorways

- ☐ Decide if the manoeuvre is really necessary.

- ☐ POSITION: Well back from the vehicle you are about to overtake.
- ☐ SPEED: Sufficient to complete the manoeuvre safely. Retain lower gear to give extra acceleration.
- ☐ LOOK: For hazards ahead and for vehicles either about to overtake or travelling in the lane you wish to enter.
- ☐ OBSERVE: Check mirrors, and over both shoulders.
- ☐ SIGNAL: In good time.
- ☐ LIFESAVER: Look behind for a final check.
- ☐ MANOEUVRE: Overtake smoothly as you may lose control of your machine if you alter direction sharply. Do not move back into the left-hand lane until it is safe.

Anticipate the following before overtaking: lane closures ahead; new traffic entering the motorway; and changing traffic situations that could affect the manoeuvre.

Always remember the lifesaver look before moving out, and ensure indicators are cancelled when the manoeuvre is completed. Never overtake on the left or weave in and out of traffic.

Night riding on motorways

- ☐ Use headlight even when carriageways are well lit.
- ☐ Do not wear tinted glasses or visors.
- ☐ Do not ride if tired.

The speed and distance of other vehicles can be deceptive at night and care needs to be taken when making riding decisions. Allow more time for all manoeuvres. Do not look directly at dazzling headlights. Stop and rest regularly at service areas.

Dealing with a breakdown

- ☐ Pull well over on to the hard shoulder.
- ☐ Follow arrows on marker posts to nearest emergency telephone and ring for assistance. These calls are free but a charge will be made to remove your machine.
- ☐ Women travelling alone may like to keep their safety helmet on and not advertise the fact they are female.

Leaving a motorway

- ☐ Use advance warning signs to plan the distance to your exit.
- ☐ Move into the left-hand lane in good time.
- ☐ Observe and signal on the approach to the first count-down marker.
- ☐ After the count-down markers, move into the deceleration lane.
- ☐ Slow down in preparation for the exit road.

Move into the left-hand lane a good distance before your exit, and do not cross more than one lane at a time. Observe and signal before changing lanes. Check the speedometer on your machine after entering the deceleration lane. Many slip roads end in sharp bends and, after travelling at high speed, a rider's judgement may be affected. Watch for advisory speed signs and comply.

Night riding

Lights at night

- ☐ Check lights are working properly.
- ☐ Keep lights and reflective lights clean.
- ☐ Headlight must be correctly aligned.

- ☐ Dip headlight when necessary.
- ☐ Dip your headlight earlier for oncoming traffic before entering a left-hand bend.

Lights fulfil two functions. They enable a rider to see, and be seen. It is an offence to ride a machine if the lights are not working properly. Replace faulty bulbs immediately, and remember an incorrectly adjusted headlamp can dazzle other road users.

Speed at night

- ☐ Ride at a speed at which you can stop safely in the length of road illuminated by the headlamp of your machine.
- ☐ Think ahead and anticipate unseen hazards.
- ☐ Slow down before entering bends.

The speed of other vehicles can be difficult to estimate at night. On dark rainy nights visibility can be as poor as in foggy conditions. Never wear tinted or so-called night driving glasses.

Use of horn at night

It is an offence to use the horn at night between 11.30pm and 7.00am in a built-up area when your machine is moving.

Observation

Take effective rear observation before:

- ☐ Any riding action.
- ☐ Changing position or direction.
- ☐ Overtaking.
- ☐ Slowing.
- ☐ Stopping.

Motorcycles are a third of the width of a car and are not always easily seen. Riders must observe and read the road ahead. Mirrors have blind spots, so always check over the shoulder before moving out. Never forget the lifesaver look.

Parking

Where to park

- ☐ Park in a legal place.
- ☐ Park in a safe place.
- ☐ Park in a convenient place.
- ☐ Park parallel to the kerb on a central stand and on level firm ground.

A motorcycle needs the same amount of parking space as a car. The Highway Code states where to avoid parking.

Parking at night

- ☐ Park on the left-hand side of the road unless in a one-way street.
- ☐ Parked motor vehicles must show lights unless in a built-up area.
- ☐ Do not park within 15 metres of a road junction.

Passing stationary vehicles

- ☐ Look ahead and decide if it is safe to pass.
- ☐ Where there is not enough room, wait well back.
- ☐ Signal if needed.
- ☐ When turning right after passing parked vehicles, reinforce the indicator signal with the appropriate arm signal.
- ☐ Give a wide berth to all parked vehicles and allow for unexpected hazards.

☐ Do not pull in until there is room to do so safely.

Give way to oncoming traffic when there is not enough room to overtake stationary vehicles safely. If in doubt, wait and give way. Allow a good clearance when passing parked vehicles in case a child runs out, the vehicle begins to move or a door is opened carelessly. Do not squeeze between parked cars and oncoming traffic and always check it is safe before pulling back in. When there are several parked vehicles, do not weave in and out.

Pillion passengers

Legal requirements

☐ Learner riders must not carry pillion passengers.

☐ Pillion passengers must wear safety helmets.

How stability is affected

☐ Riders must make allowance for a pillion passenger when turning corners.

☐ Stopping distances increase when a pillion passenger is carried.

Pillion passengers must sit securely astride the machine and close behind the rider. The performance and handling characteristics of machines, especially small ones, are affected when a passenger is carried and, for this reason, learner riders are not allowed to carry another person on their machine. Pillion passengers must not distract the rider in any way.

Rain

Rain can reduce visibility substantially, and riders should ensure their goggles or visors do not mist up. Spray from lorries is a particular hazard. Gloves are available with suede fingers for wiping wet visors and there are anti-mist sprays available at car and motorcycle accessory shops. (See section on waterproof clothing.)

Pillion passengers must not distract the rider in any way.

Road surfaces

Avoid riding or braking on or in:

- ☐ Manhole covers and drains.
- ☐ The gutter.
- ☐ White lines, 'cats eyes' and metal road studs.
- ☐ Mud, loose chippings, leaves and cow muck.

Riders of two-wheeled machines depend on balance to maintain stability, and must take account of changing road surfaces. Watch for road debris which gathers in the gutters and beware of adverse cambers.

Keep away from road markings which can be as slippery as ice, and overbanding where the surface has been patched up after road works. Diesel may be spilled by other vehicles on corners, garage forecourts and the approach to roundabouts, increasing the likelihood of skidding. Ride extra carefully after rain following a dry spell, because oil and fuel deposited on the road floats, making it treacherous.

Separation distances

Overall stopping distances in good conditions

- ☐ 30mph – 75feet; 23metres
- ☐ 40mph – 120feet; 36metres
- ☐ 50mph – 175feet; 53metres
- ☐ 60mph – 240feet; 73metres
- ☐ 70mph – 315feet; 96metres

Hang back and do not ride closely behind other road users. If vehicles in front of you stop suddenly, you must have sufficient space to stop safely. Allow double the distance in wet weather conditions, and in foggy or icy weather reduce speed further according to the severity of the road conditions.

On the open road on a dry day, leave a two-second gap or one metre for each mph of speed. On motorways, in good conditions, when riding at 70mph, keep the equivalent of the distance between two marker posts behind the vehicle in front.

When travelling in a group, ride in a stepped formation, that is, avoid riding in each other's wheel tracks, leaving a good distance between each rider, according to road and weather conditions.

Signals

Arm signals

- ☐ Right arm extended for turning right.
- ☐ Left arm extended for turning left.

- ☐ Right arm up and down before slowing and stopping.

A signal should be given, when necessary, to warn other road users of a planned manoeuvre. Signal your intentions in good time, especially when changing lanes on a motorway. Riders using indicators should give a secondary arm signal where visibility allows but not in fast-moving traffic when the throttle needs to be maintained. Cancel indicators when a manoeuvre is completed.

Signals given to or by others

- ☐ Do not flash your headlamp at other road users unless to warn them of your presence.
- ☐ When other road users signal, act on the signal only if it is safe.
- ☐ Do not beckon pedestrians or other drivers. They must make their own decisions.

Apart from warning, there is no recognised meaning of a flashing headlight. You may confuse or endanger other road users by 'flashing' them on.

Skidding

Causes of skidding:

- ☐ Accelerating sharply.
- ☐ Braking sharply.
- ☐ Cornering sharply.

Skidding is caused by rider error, not icy roads and slippery surfaces.

Factors which affect road holding:

- ☐ Wet roads.
- ☐ Ice and snow.
- ☐ Loose road surfaces.

- ☐ Uneven loads.
- ☐ Worn or wrongly inflated tyres.

On slippery roads, riders can double the grip of their tyres by reducing their speed by half. Watch out for loose road surfaces. Wet roads may be covered in mud which can affect the stability of your machine, especially when braking.

How to avoid skidding

- ☐ Anticipate hazards and plan well ahead.
- ☐ Maintain your brakes properly.
- ☐ Replace worn or damaged tyres.
- ☐ Check tyre pressures frequently.
- ☐ Brake progressively on the straight when the machine is upright.
- ☐ Accelerate, brake and corner gently.
- ☐ Drive at a safe speed according to the road and weather conditions.
- ☐ Do not apply the clutch until just before stopping.

Skidding . . .

On a motorcycle, the front brake is designed for maximum braking and the rear brake for maximum grip. On a dry surface, apply 75% front brake with 25% back brake. On wet roads this alters to 50-50. On a very slippery surface, leave the front brake alone and, if absolutely necessary, apply the back brake gently.

Should the rear wheel lock and begin to slide, to regain control ease off the brakes immediately. A locked front wheel usually results in the rider coming off. The risk of locking the brakes is diminished by cadence braking on the rear brake. This means applying, releasing, applying, releasing the rear brake in rapid cadence instead of progressively braking.

Aquaplaning

Avoid aquaplaning by:

- ☐ Reducing speed below 50mph in wet weather.
- ☐ Ensuring the tyres have an adequate depth of tread.

When tyres are turning in wet weather, a ridge of water may build underneath them. The higher the speed, the more water, until eventually there is a film of water between the tyres and the road. The rider may be unaware of the problem until applying the brakes – which will not have any effect.

Snow and ice

Rules for riding in snow or ice

- ☐ Remove snow from indicators and lights.
- ☐ Check cables have not frozen on.
- ☐ Clear snow from under wheel arches and around tyres.
- ☐ Use the highest gear you can, probably second, to move off.

- ☐ Operate all riding controls gently.
- ☐ Wear warm and waterproof clothing.
- ☐ Lack of tyre noise may warn of black ice.
- ☐ Keep your feet up to help balance.

When snow is falling or conditions are icy, stay off the roads unless your journey is absolutely essential. Listen to local radio stations, or contact one of the motoring organisations for accurate information about road conditions. Hard snow gives no grip; soft snow a little more. Make use of engine braking and avoid using the brakes. Stopping distances can increase by 10 times on icy roads. Select a lower gear before climbing hills and stay in it, and also a lower gear before travelling downhill.

Speed and speed limits

The national speed limits for cars and motorcycles are:

- ☐ 70mph on motorways.
- ☐ 70mph on dual carriageways.
- ☐ 60mph on single carriageways unless signs indicate otherwise.
- ☐ 30mph in built-up areas where there is street lighting and in the absence of signs to the contrary.
- ☐ 20mph in zones (usually residential) approved by the Secretary of State for Transport.

These are the maximum speed limits allowed on roads in the United Kingdom. In many instances, it will be unsafe and unwise to ride as fast as the limit allows. Reduce speed when riding conditions are poor and at night when judgement may be impaired. Blue circular signs with a speed limit indicate a minimum speed and are found where there are long underpasses and tunnels. Vehicles towing a trailer must comply with a maximum speed limit of 60mph.

Tyres

Legal requirements for tyres

- ☐ A visible tread pattern on a moped.
- ☐ At least 1.6mm of tread covering the circumference and 75% of the width of the tyre on a motorcycle.
- ☐ Tyres must be inflated to the correct pressure.
- ☐ There must be no cuts, bulges, breaks in fabric or ply structure exposed.

Although 1.6 millimetres of tread depth is the legal minimum except for mopeds, which must have a visible tread pattern, it is inadvisable to allow the tread to wear below 3 millimetres. Braking distance is adversely affected as tread depth is reduced. Correctly inflated tyres will last longer. Check pressures when tyres are cold and, if riding long distances at speed, increase the pressure in the tyres according to manufacturer's requirements. Before riding any machine or vehicle check the tyres for wear or damage. Start at the valve and check all the way round, especially for damage which may have occurred to the tyre walls.

Tyre safety rules

- ☐ Fit tyres of the size and type recommended by the manufacturer.
- ☐ Check tyres and replace when necessary.
- ☐ Have wheels balanced and trued regularly when the machine is serviced.
- ☐ Correctly inflate tyres and replace valve caps.
- ☐ Ensure repairs are done only by a reputable tyre specialist.

Worn tyres can kill and maim.

Brakes do not stop the motorcycle: they only slow the

wheels. Tyres stop the machine, and to be effective they must grip the road surface. Poorly maintained tyres will be unable to perform this function.

Avoid damaging tyres against kerbs or pot-holes. Do not accelerate, corner or brake sharply. Skidding can reduce the life of tyres and, in some cases, of the rider! New tyres should be 'bedded in' at low speeds for the first 50 miles.

Burst tyres

- ☐ Hold handlebars firmly.
- ☐ Do not apply the brakes.
- ☐ Allow the machine to roll to a halt if possible.

Tyres are your only contact with the road – look after them.

Wind

These are the rules for riding in windy weather conditions:

- ☐ Slow down to increase the stability of the machine.
- ☐ Watch out for gateways and exposed places.
- ☐ Make allowances for side winds when passing long vehicles.

Motorcyclists are vulnerable to side winds and gusts. On motorways and dual carriageways, beware of drag from articulated lorries and other large vehicles.

Zebra (pedestrian) and pelican crossings

Pedestrian crossings

- ☐ Watch for advance warning signs of crossings.
- ☐ Stop and give way to pedestrians crossing.
- ☐ Slow and be prepared to stop for people waiting to cross. Stop at the 'Give Way' line.

Make allowances for side winds when passing long vehicles.

- ☐ Do not park on or near the zig-zag lines.
- ☐ Do not overtake within the zig-zag lines on the approach to a pedestrian crossing.

Pedestrians using a pedestrian crossing have an absolute right of way and drivers must stop and wait until pedestrians are off the crossing. Where there is a central refuge, treat both halves as a separate crossing. An arm signal will give pedestrians confirmation you are slowing down or stopping but do not wave anybody across in case another driver or rider has not seen them.

Pelican crossings

- ☐ STOP if the lights are red.
- ☐ STOP if the lights are flashing amber AND people are crossing.

- ☐ STOP when the lights are on amber, unless to do so would cause an accident.
- ☐ GO if the lights are green and the way is clear.
- ☐ GO if the lights are flashing amber and people are no longer on the crossing.
- ☐ Do not park or overtake within the zig-zag lines.

A staggered pelican (pedestrian controlled) crossing with a central refuge is treated as two separate crossings. Watch for pedestrians pressing the button as the lights may change quickly.

By the Same Authors

HOW TO PASS YOUR DRIVING TEST
An easy-to-read handbook that contains all the information learner drivers need to pass their test. It includes the actual words used by an examiner and details the new D.S.A. recommended syllabus for driving instructors. This second edition has been enlarged and updated to include recent changes made to the driving test and a useful addition is a section for newly qualified drivers.

DRIVING TEST QUESTIONS AND ANSWERS
An invaluable guide for learner riders and drivers who want an easy way of testing their knowledge of the Highway Code. The 201 questions are based on those most commonly asked during driving tests and appear on left-hand pages with the answers given on the facing page. Other useful information on motoring matters is included.

BE AN ADVANCED DRIVER
This book is essential reading for everyone wishing to improve their driving to an advanced standard. It contains detailed information on all aspects of safe driving including correct motorway procedures, dealing with floods, towing a trailer, burst tyres and making an insurance claim against another driver. This is an extremely useful reference book and should be kept in a handy place by all motorists. An ideal gift for drivers.

